I0820222

SCENE

A MEMOIR

ABEL FERRARA

SIMON & SCHUSTER

NEW YORK AMSTERDAM/ANTWERP LONDON

TORONTO SYDNEY/MELBOURNE NEW DELHI

Simon & Schuster
1230 Avenue of the Americas
New York, NY 10020

First Simon & Schuster hardcover edition October 2025

Interior design by Carly Loman

Manufactured in the United States of America

1 3 5 7 9 10 8 6 4 2

Library of Congress Control Number is available.

ISBN 978-1-6680-9767-0
ISBN 978-1-6680-9769-4 (ebook)

For Endira, Lucy, and Anna
and their mothers, Nancy and Cristina

SCENE

COULD THIS BE LOVE

NADIA

We broke up on December 7, 1974, Pearl Harbor Day. We had played out the string of this relationship. Nadia and I were living in an old house in Nyack on the Hudson River, a forty-minute drive north of Manhattan but as far away as the moon. We were in that dark place for college sweethearts when college is over. I was spending days commuting into the city, trying to find a paying job in the film business, willing to do anything. I was in no-man's-land, either make a living in the real world as a filmmaker or work the rest of my life driving a scrap metal truck for my father or a garbage truck for my uncle. I was doing it part-time, out of family responsibility and because I needed the cash. Everyone I knew was watching, seeing if I could make that leap from university hotshot to life as a working director.

Nadia had made up her mind about her future. She wanted out. She had been the star of my graduate film *Could This Be Love*, a twenty-six-minute color sync sound film which was to be our ticket to paradise. She was the cool blonde playing the lead. She wanted to be an actress, but she didn't have the fire that was raging inside of me. We finished the film in the summer and now it was the dead of winter. I came home exhausted from work and she just laid it on me. She was in love with a friend of mine, a successful NYC photographer who she was modeling on and off for, with a big studio downtown and an apartment on Central Park South.

"You want to leave right now?"

"Yes."

"Tonight?"

"Yes, I want to be with him tonight."

"It can't wait till after Christmas? My mother and sisters already bought you a present." No, it couldn't.

It was her apartment, in theory, that we were sharing the rent on. So in the face of her honesty, in the early darkness of December, I put on the only suit I had, a blue velvet one I bought for someone's wedding, and picked up my Goya guitar and the large 16mm film can that held my university thesis. We had spent a year of our lives on it, plus a few thousand dollars of my mother's money and the blood and favors of everyone we knew. *Could This Be Love*, right. I got in my car feeling released, intoxicated, jet-propelled into my future and drove off deeper into the suburban heartland of Rockland County, Pearl River, to another big old white house like the one I had just left.

Dennis was an artist and classical piano player who was an actor in the film. It was his house, and when he saw me standing there he began laughing hysterically in that high-pitched voice of his. He knew the whole story without asking and led me to a monk-style room on the second floor with a desk and a bed and a window looking out into the backwoods. I felt good, thankful to have friends like him and a place to begin again, until the middle of the night when I woke up in tears, shattered by the heartbreak of losing my first true love. We had had our ups and downs and mini-breakups over the past five years but she was everything a dude from Peekskill could imagine in a girlfriend. Tall, beautiful, from an aristocratic Russian family with European manners, a light-year from the blue-collar Southern Italian war zone I came from. We met as freshmen at Rockland Community College, which coming from Northern Westchester was like studying at the Sorbonne. Now that life was over and I knew it, but to deal with it was a new lesson in extended pain. Dylan's new album came out, *Blood On the Tracks.* Dennis had some nice speakers and a turntable and like every brokenhearted motherfucker I listened to that record a million times.

9 LIVES

MATTY THE HORSE

Matty Ianniello's office was in Midtown Manhattan in the 50s off Sixth Avenue, on a block full of the highest rents per square foot in the world. In 1975 Matty the Horse, as he was called, ruled Midtown. The go-go club scene was in full swing, along with the X-rated theaters. That was the legitimate side. The high-end gambling parlors, the second-story shit, Wall Street swindling, phony credit cards, and any hustle you can think of were also his. Like Walken says in *King of New York*, "A nickel bag gets sold in the park, I want in." And that's how it was, anything shady going down in Midtown, he was your partner. This was a golden age for these guys, ten years before Giuliani and any kind of real government crackdown, and a few years after Coppola's *Godfather*.

Matty wasn't your average wise guy, you didn't get to where he got by just breaking heads, you needed the brains and the charisma to go with the willingness to adhere to the code. The real scary guys were those who came back from the war and hit the streets with all that good stuff they learned, how to use explosives and how to really handle weapons. Matty was a hero in World War II, served in the Pacific theater with the medals of bravery to show for it. The introduction was from my father, who was a friend of his in another lifetime. Tired of watching me struggle and fail through a series of potential investors, my father figured it was time to introduce me to the people who could really help me.

The slick lobby was guarded by uniformed doormen and the elevator took me to a long polished corridor leading to a big mahogany door. Inside was an office that appeared to be from another building, with some secondhand furniture in what might have been a waiting room and, behind a funky glass counter, a heavily made-up woman acting out the role of receptionist. It was five in the afternoon, which is when their office opened, just as the rest of the building was getting ready to go home. She told me to go inside and wait in his office. Nobody used his name.

His office was a big table with nothing on it, two chairs at either end and a forgotten filing cabinet in the corner. After a few minutes Matty walked in and sat across from me. He looked liked Luca Brasi from Coppola's film and spoke so deep and gravelly that if you weren't raised on it you wouldn't understand one word. Years later in the same office he would hand me the FBI indictment against him, pages of transcribed wiretaps, asking me, "What did they say I did?" Reading what some middle American FBI guys thought they heard on that wire was hysterical, except that he went to jail for it.

But back then nobody was putting him away, nobody was even trying. He sat in that chair across from me without a worry in the world. He was a big dude, not fat but big. If it came to guns, fine, but he could handle himself without one. He was sharp, street-smart. I would come to learn he had a gift for sizing up a situation, making a plan, and acting on it in the same moment. He listened to my pitch, which was basically asking for money for my new film, and said come back in a week and he would let me know.

It doesn't take more than a few positive words when you are at this stage of asking for money. Even now I can turn "I will let you know" into accepting an Academy Award or two. Mark Twain said, "The worst things in my life never happened." Well you can add the best things to that too. But in my business you'll use anything for a bit of traction.

It was February in 1975 and NYC was cold and dangerous. My first apartment on 15th and Union Square was a studio in a classy old building with marble pillars, one small room with a bigger bathroom and strangely an even bigger closet. Union Square, which was to be my neighborhood for the next twenty-five years, was off limits after dark back then. It is the first main subway stop from Brooklyn and all the young thugs made it their own. Nighttime was Dobermans barking and occasional gunshots and I don't think I ever went in there after the streetlights went on.

The city was going bankrupt, the cops were on strike, and a fire had wiped out telephone service in my part of the East Side. There were a couple of AT&T trucks filled with pay phones parked on Third Avenue, and that was it for communication out, communication in was zero. I remember trying the phone in my apartment incessantly for three weeks before one day I picked it up and heard a dial tone, a spiritual moment.

Being alone in NYC for the first time is exhilarating but diabolically lonely, the alone you feel surrounded by 10 million people, with no friends, no money, and a heart still in a thousand pieces. My longtime composer Joe Delia's brother Frank shared the photo studio on Fifth and 13th with the guy who stole my girl, so what used to be a hangout was now enemy territory. Everyone I knew still lived upstate, so NYC at night was only mine. I learned where to walk and where not to, the best and cheapest pizza by the slice, the bars that would let you in to hear music without having to buy a drink.

I got some kind of flu and was laid up with nothing but tap water and change to call my mother from the phone truck, when I heard a knock at my door. It was my uncle Bobo, my father's younger brother, my godfather and confidant throughout my childhood. He was a sweet and gentle soul and I loved and adored him. How he found my place or got past the doorman was part of his mystique. He was doing business in town and wanted to make sure I was all right. I was recovered enough to go with him to Pete's Tavern, a classic expensive restaurant down the block. He ordered all my favorite food and just smoked a cigarette as I ate everything that was put in front of me. He lived up in Bridgeport, Connecticut, another funky destination like Peekskill, part of my family's diaspora from the Bronx.

He said, "Your father is not happy." He didn't say disappointed, but that's what it really was. My father loved me, his only son, too much to say it, so he left it to his kid brother to tell me that broke and unemployed at twenty-four, with a useless degree and few prospects, wasn't exactly the vision he had for me. When I was in my final year of university I took the law boards, an entrance exam, more as a lark but also to stay close to a school's free film equipment, my lifeline. I took a Black Beauty and miraculously did well. I envisioned going to law school and emerging three years later with a degree and a few more films made, a superhero independent filmmaker entertainment lawyer. I was brought back to earth by my friend's brother, a lawyer. When I said I was applying he said, "I thought you were going to be a filmmaker." I said I would do both and he laughed at me, saying,

"The first two years of law school I didn't have time to read the newspaper." I took his word for it. But now my uncle was bringing it up again. He put an offer on the table. There was a law school in Connecticut near him and he knew people there that could get me in. He would pay for my education, get me my own place near the school, and give me money to live on. How many people have uncles like that? I said no, I am making a film, I have a plan. He said, "It would make your mother happy." That was a low blow, but still I refused.

My mother was not Italian. She was a beautiful Irish woman, blue-eyed, blond-haired, every bit the Marilyn Monroe to my father's Joe DiMaggio, which was the template for these interracial marriages. My aunts and uncles all went the safe route and married Italians or Jews. My mother was also born in the South Bronx but she came from abject poverty, not a working-class immigrant family like my father's. She lost both her parents when she was fourteen and had to raise her younger sister and three younger brothers, with little help from her two older brothers, who were still in their teens and well on their way to being Irish drunks. Somehow she kept the family together.

As a child of welfare, the luxuries of a bourgeois housewife meant zero to her. She could appreciate the comfort zone but didn't trust it or need it. When you grow up with Christmas being a grapefruit, and an orange for your sister, it makes you grateful for what's real. For her, as long as I wasn't dead or in jail she was fine. Maybe because of the star dreams of her older brother Kenneth, a failed vaudeville song-and-dance man and my only relative that was remotely associated with show business, she got what I was shooting for. From the time I started making 8mm films as a sixteen-year-old she was there, my go-to financier, taking money out of my father's pants pocket he didn't even know he had while he was sleeping. Dorothy O'Brien was cool like that.

I went back to Matty's office and waited at the same empty desk. I could hear people talking in the other room, his business partners, guys I would get to know later, Benny Cohen, Robbie Margulies, slick dudes, perfectly manicured fingernails and razor haircuts. My father always preached to me that you can't make money with Italians, you had to stick with Jews, Italians were too resentful and jealous to get anywhere with. Then he would rattle off the names of some serious Italian gangsters, followed by a Jewish guy you never heard of. When they got to Matty it was Benny and Robbie, and now here they were. Robbie I especially grew to like. His brother owned a famous uptown steakhouse, and who knows everything that Robbie was into. He was making oil deals with the Russians and was involved in casinos in Las Vegas and Atlantic City. He was one of the few people in the world able to count cards at the blackjack table, which would have gotten him banned from his own casinos. He was the first guy I ever saw wearing gold bling around his neck, along with the rings and Rolexes they all had.

Matty came in the room, sat down, and laid out his proposal. "You know Jerry Weintraub?" Jerry Weintraub was Frank Sinatra's manager, as well as a major Hollywood producer making big-budget movies. "Jerry will fly you out to California, he will give you $500 a week and you follow him around."

"What do you mean follow him around?"

"You know, carry his bag, do what he needs you to do." This was a serious favor to extend to the son of an old friend, to take me from nowhere and propel me to the middle of that whole game. Except I wanted to make a movie, not follow some guy around, no matter who he was. I thanked him for the offer but told him again I was trying to raise $25,000 to make the film. In a prescient moment, which is what separated him from most of the others, he said, "Why do you want to ruin your father?" Then he stood up, told me to wait there, and left. Twenty-five minutes later in walked Franky C.

Franky was what they referred to as a smart guy, and for the next thirty-five years he would be my sometime manager, producer, and actor. He was someone I could always count on when I needed it most.

The breakdown is this: A smart guy is a guy who can make money. A tough guy is a leg-breaker and maybe a killer. A wise guy is a killer, a made man, and you had to be 100 percent Italian to be in that club. Gerard Damiano was a smart guy, a hairdresser from the Bronx who directed *Deep Throat* and the follow-up, *Devil in Miss Jones*, which were killing it at the box office, high up on *Variety*'s Top 50 list of the highest-grossing films. He introduced me to his producer Tommy from Miami, who was definitely a tough guy and was the one who ended up making all the money. When I told him I needed some help to get in the business he turned cold and said, "You're not thinking about ripping us off, right?"

"No, I just want to make a movie."

A meeting was set for ten o'clock the following night, which was mid-morning to these guys. Lino's is a restaurant on 35th Street buried deep in the Garment District. The place was empty except for the maître d' who, when I told him who I was meeting, sat me in a side booth. Tommy shows up looking slick with the go-to Julius Caesar haircut, his wide collar open over wider lapels, with a Kim Novak look-alike walking alongside. 1975 was the real fashion year for ridiculous-looking shit but at least she could make it work. I was too wound up to eat and said I would order later. He just had a drink and waited while they brought her out a dish of veal parmigiana with a side of spaghetti. She starts eating like it's the last meal of her life.

After an awkward ten minutes he says, "Is your guy coming or not?" Just then a dude who was sitting at the bar in the corner comes up to us. He is dressed in a dark conservative suit with a dark shirt, no tie, pretty much like I was. With a Hester Street accent, as opposed to the Broome Street one that Matty had, he says, "My friend is on his way." He goes back to the bar and we wait for what seems like an eternity, then Franky C shows up. He is also dressed in the fashion, only he's wearing a tie. Franky believed in ties. I once saw him buy a thousand dollars' worth of them while waiting for a plane. "It's the topper," he used to say. Franky is of medium height and back then he weighed close to four hundred pounds. He sits down next to Tommy and the guy at the bar, whose name is Z, comes over uninvited and sits next to me. There's some small talk and then we get down to business.

Tommy starts explaining how it works, what us creative types have to look forward to for the rest of our lives. We come in with the ideas, the energy, do most of the work and for their investment the financiers figure whatever money gets made is theirs. We keep the glory. These were gangsters, so they weren't obliged to couch this any way but direct. Pointing his finger at me, Tommy laid out the next fifty years of my movie business existence. "Who gets ripped off? It's guys like him who get ripped off." It was the last sentence that got Z's attention. He looked right at Tommy. "He's from our office. Nobody rips him off."

Z was the real deal, intense, with a thin wiry body and narrow eyes. Downtown he was known as the Chinaman. Focusing on him for the first time, Tommy got the picture, and he didn't like it. He was stuck between Kim Novak and a wall on one side and a four-hundred-pound dude on the other. Across the table was me, a long-haired, crazed maybe-director, and Z, who if Tommy didn't know before he did now. But Tommy stays cool, turns, puts his hand in front of his mouth and whispers in Franky's ear, "So who are you with?"

"The fat guy," Franky says, the term they used for Matty. Tommy is incredulous but relieved because he works for him too. "You're with him and you're asking me for money? Why don't you give him the money yourselves?" Franky says, "I'd rather buy him a house."

In the end it was my father who put up the 25k. The deal he made with Matty was that he would front the money and Matty would watch over the production and keep an eye on me and make sure no one bothered us. So now Franky C, his pal Cha Cha, and the rest of that gang were my producers.

Nicky St. John, my screenwriter and filmmaking partner, had just come back from Germany with a master's in philosophy from the University of Würzburg. We were ready to start our careers, and now we belonged to something. We had a start date to make a 35mm film with a clear distribution plan. NYC was no longer a fortress of closed doors. We were hooked up. Mulberry Street between Hester and Canal was our new stomping ground and shooting location. No more steady diets of Stromboli pizza with that syrupy fake cola, although if it wasn't for the generosity of those young Sicilians who ran the pizzeria on 13th and University we would have already starved to death. When you're sitting at Umberto's and Matty comes in and tells the waiter he's got your check, New York becomes what everyone dreams it can be.

Our production office was uptown, Mambo Hy Talent Agency between 53rd and 54th, a five-room apartment overlooking Broadway. You could look across Seventh Avenue and see the Stage Deli on one corner and the Carnegie on the other. This was no downtown scene, this was Broadway and all the show people and ballplayers and serious mob guys were right there, and Franky C knew them all, from Jackie Wilson to Clay Cole to Tiny Tim.

Mambo Hy was the agency for the girls who danced in the topless clubs. They had made-up names like Smokey and Lola and Gemini and were from every walk of life. Some were students working their way through school, digging the independence from their families that that kind of money gave them. Go-go clubs ruled back then, they were like theater, and the audience wasn't just guys in trench coats. Limousines full of fashionable people would pull up to clubs called The Carousel, The Playpen, and The Pussycat Lounge. The girls also worked the seedy bars filled with seedy people in places like Lake Ronkonkoma or out in Jersey somewhere, and because they all belonged to Matty there was some semblance of order. He was a security blanket that stretched far into the boroughs.

When it came time to cast the film we did not want professional porno actors or actresses. We had convinced ourselves we were making a real film so we were looking for real people. We must have been pretty persuasive about the validity of our movie because we attracted three of Mambo Hy's best dancers for our leads. Chantal may or may not have come from France but she was a killer, long black curly hair, an intriguing damaged face. Ava was a big athletic blonde who could have had a chance in Hollywood. Joy was Black, with a strong gay side like a lot of the dancers. She was over-the-top beautiful, funny, outrageous, somehow holding on to her innocence. I've never seen anyone with her color skin. It was amber and glowed in the right light from the right camera angle. They say you have to love them to direct them, so I had no excuses for this film. Their backstories, which you got in dribs and drabs, were astounding and left them streetwise and tough. If we were only smart enough to film their real lives we would have made a great movie.

The script bounced us all around location-wise

so we figured we would start in Frank Delia's photo studio for the exposition stuff and then move to the apartment Cha Cha had above his cafe on Mulberry Street, another "safe" environment. We could delude ourselves that we were making *Salò* or *Last Tango* or a Fassbinder movie, but this was a Triple X movie, real sex, cum shots, and people were getting busted for that as well as making fortunes. Who cares? We were making our first 35mm feature and I wasn't even twenty-five.

Shooting actual sex is not so simple. When approaching a film you have to invent a method of shooting to capture the action inherent to that project. You discover it shot to shot. There is no other way. In the middle of figuring it all out the one actual porno actor we cast couldn't get it up. That's a disaster. I am giving this guy 300 bucks, a small fortune, to fuck what is essentially our girlfriends, and he can't do it. It's an insult. Cha Cha and Franky C are sitting downstairs in beach chairs playing producers, and they're not happy to hear that we're about to blow a day's shoot. Between me freaking out and the actor realizing exactly who he's pissing off, the dude makes the brilliant move of slipping out the bathroom window, down the back fire escape, and off somewhere into the Lower East Side.

I grew up choosing up sides or playing rock, paper, scissors, all games with your fingers. Drawing straws was something out of a World War II movie but that's how we did it. It was me, Frank Delia, and a couple of the crew guys, and I got the short one.

The scene was the story of Job that Nicky St. John lifted from the Bible, how the two daughters had to do their father to procreate the race. So they put some talcum powder on my head and I acted like I was sleeping while Chantal and Ava worked out on me.

We made the day and everybody was happy, only I had a mother and now three daughters and I have to live with that. My mother raised me to respect women and respect myself, and in this film we crossed that line. To continue to make hard-core movies was not us, it was against our nature, so we stopped after one.

BAYBI DAY

Dusty was an Elle Macpherson look-alike from Long Island, who when doing her G-string thing in one of the Midtown clubs was probably the best show on Broadway. She wasn't looking for a Tony award, just her college tuition. One day she was warring with Franky C over some minimal amount of money owed to her. They were going back and forth when Robbie Margulies handed Frank the phone, saying, "Tell them we are good with the million for Sinatra, but he has to play the whole week, not just Labor Day Weekend." I sat and watched as Franky took care of Dusty's seven-dollar bump-up and Sinatra's million-dollar contract simultaneously.

Nicky was in a back room writing *Fear City* as a $100,000 follow-up to *9 Lives*. It was a big leap for us budget-wise. We were homeless, living in the office of the go-go agency or crashing down in Franky's studio. The movie was done and we were just waiting for it to come out and turn my father's 25k investment into the millions *Behind the Green Door* or *Debbie Does Dallas* were making. We had a long wait. But these fantasies are what keep you going when you're young and dumb and yet to get the message about how the film business really works. I still keep the breakout fantasy intact. The idea of pulling together a minimum investment, shooting the shit out of the movie, and then having the whole world go to watch it is one dream I am not giving up.

One night me, Nicky, and Frank Delia went into a place in the village called The Purple Onion that was a folk club back in the '60s, but in the fall of '75 was a topless bar. The West Village by then was basically just 42nd Street South, with pimps, hustlers, street dealers, and their prey. Playing the Mambo Hy card we managed to talk our way inside but had to pay for the drinks. It was a Sunday night and the club was pretty much empty. We had just enough money for one beer for the three of us, nothing to tip the dancer. She came out onto the small dark stage and my life turned upside down. She was medium height and her breasts weren't big, which wasn't rare because instant breast jobs weren't the rage yet. She was feline and fine and looked like the most beautiful version of Jagger you ever saw. She didn't dance as much as just be there, sensing the music with a spaced-out stare into the beyond.

When I got back to the office I went right to the

big board to see who danced at The Onion that shift and it was Sabrina. Later, after I got to know her, I found her real name was Pamela, soon to be changed to Baybi Day, and that she remembered us sitting in the club in our leather jackets with our long hair and thought we looked cool, different. Franky C's partner at the agency told me she was a space case from near Baltimore somewhere, and what did I see in that skinny freak? I just checked out where she was dancing next. It was the following Sunday night at a club in the Bronx. When Sunday came it was pouring rain and I had no money. The club might as well have been on another planet.

At three o'clock in the morning I couldn't take it anymore. Frank Delia came out of his darkroom where he was souping his own negatives. I asked if he wanted to come and he said, "Shit, why not." He barely pulled together our subway fare, never mind an umbrella, and we headed for the train. The subway line went right through Apache country, East Harlem and the South Bronx. Somewhere north of 115th Street a guy stood up with his back to the door, took out a knife and started speaking to it. The few of us on the train neither moved or stared, and at the next stop the doors opened, he looked around, put the knife back in his pocket and left and the train rumbled on.

Who knew exactly where the club was, GPS was in some sci-fi future. This was the era when people would actually get lost, in fact half the people were usually lost and asking for directions. I had some of my best life experiences trying to find where I was going. We found the club easy though, because this was all about fate.

She was doing her set, again not really dancing, just swaying, neither acknowledging the audience nor appearing interested in making money. The girls picked their own music, so it went from disco to pure heaven, early Temptations, the Stones, "Honey Bee" by Gloria Gaynor. There was another long-haired young guy in the club who turned out to be her boyfriend, so my dream of waltzing her out of there and into my arms was not happening that night. As a teenager upstate I once tried my go-to line on a twenty-two-year-old. "Hey, do you have a boyfriend?" She educated me. "Abel, all good-looking girls have boyfriends."

Pamela finished her set, then miraculously asked if we needed a ride back to Manhattan. Mario, who I got to know later on and was a good guy, had a big black Oldsmobile. I sat in the front, her beside me but hugging up to him, and we drove back downtown through the rain with the radio playing and no one speaking a word. I think I made *Driller Killer* just because I needed to get next to her. The search is never ending, but like Godard's Anna Karina when you find her you know it. Zoe, Béatrice Dalle, Lili Taylor, Asia, Juliette Binoche, I didn't marry any of them like Godard or Rossellini, and most of the time the relationship was professional, but the obsession was the same.

MY FATHER

He bought a 1959 Pontiac Star Chief that looked like a silver spaceship. Later on, when I was shooting the pilot of *Crime Story*, a TV show set in the early '60s, Michael Mann said to me, "When it comes to the cars, stick with 1957." But '59 wasn't bad either. In the Morris Park section of the Bronx it was a brand-new Cadillac or nothing. My uncles all drove Caddies, whether they could afford them or not. My father was the exception. He'd drive Buicks or Oldsmobiles, the drabber the better, because he didn't want anyone thinking he could afford something more. He didn't want anyone being jealous over something he had that they didn't, or worse, thinking they could borrow money from him. But now he was broke and owed a lot of money to some not-good people. In desperation he got the car on credit in order to raise the money. His thinking was no one lends money to someone who needs it. People only lend you money when you are rolling.

I loved and adored that car. There was more chrome and shit on the dashboard than a hundred cars today have on them anywhere, if chrome hasn't been outlawed altogether. Me and my friends would just sit in it for hours. That lasted about a week, till one morning I came downstairs on the way to school and found the car smashed to shit, windshield barely there, tires slashed, its beautiful poetic lines destroyed by whoever it was my father owed money to. My old man was a bar owner and a bookmaker, mostly a bookmaker, and it's a good business unless you start being your own customer. The odds are with the house, always, which is why I won't even play for a dollar or buy a lottery ticket or any bullshit like that. It's a losing proposition.

Like all real addicts my old man would have long periods when he would not play, just take the action, make his commission, and all would be cool in the world of my mother and sister and me. More than cool, we would be living the high life, the only people in the neighborhood who had ever seen a plane, never mind flying back and forth to Miami in the wintertime. Real gamblers only get the kick when everything they have is on the line. If you play like that it ends in smashed cars, and me coming home from second grade to friends of my father's I didn't know playing cards at our kitchen table, there to protect us from his other friends, who had threatened to off his wife and kids if they didn't get their money.

One of my first memories in life was in a different apartment, I was around four years old and just learning to open the front door. That was my thing, whenever someone knocked I would run and unlock it. This time it was two NYC police detectives, their shoes in one hand and their pistols in the other. They were there for their payoff from the local bookie, who happened to be my father, and when you were late with it that's how they came, real quiet with their shoes off. My mother hustled me into the kitchen while my father took the cops into the hallway to make the payment. She tried to tell me they were his friends. It was the first time I saw my mother cry. But now, a few years later, she wasn't crying. She'd had enough of this primal greaseball bullshit. She wanted out, which in this hood in the '50s was a pretty liberated act.

My father owned a bar near what would become the Throgs Neck Bridge out in the middle of nowhere, because they weren't looking for customers, it was just a front for their gambling operation. The routine was, at the end of the night my father's partner left first and my old man would stay and lock up. This night, under heavy pressure of the gambling debt he had no chance of paying, my mother leaving with his two kids, or worse someone actually hurting us, I guess he saw only one way out and emptied the prescription bottle of barbiturates he was abusing and washed them down with plenty of Seagram's 7. His, and my, one-in-a-million shot came in that night. His partner left his house keys at the bar, came back to get them, and saved my father's life.

Coming back from school the next day all my uncle told me was that my father was sick and had to go to the hospital, and that me and my sister were going with my mother to live at her sister's house in Peekskill. We stayed with my aunt and my German uncle and my cousin Bobby, a boy a little older who was like a big brother to me. This was rural life in the most northern part of Westchester, a small house on a cul-de-sac, my uncle with a regular job as a crew dispatcher on the railroad. It was a 180 degree change from the circus life with my crazy relatives in our Pelham Park section of the Bronx.

A week or so later my father came, walking a mile from the train station, to ask for his family back. Thankfully my mother agreed. This was his bottom, anyone's, and he changed. We got a little two-bedroom bungalow of our own where he had to walk to work as the bartender on the day shift of a cowboy bar in Montrose, the next town over, for 90 bucks a week. I am sure the tips in Cooks Tavern were negligible, but he had his life and his family back, and we had a father who would be home every evening at the same time. It was a beautiful period for all of us. My mother was working as a waitress in a luncheonette, and for the first time we were enrolled in a non-Catholic school. I was no longer in a madhouse of fifty boys, white shirts and ties, bouncing off the walls, under the whip of the young nuns. Now, with caring teachers, the world of science and math were opened to me, along with a library and people patient enough to teach me how to use it. It was a revelation. We lived near a Carvel Ice Cream stand and a drive-in theater, the go-to family event of the week in the summertime, showing movies like *The Bellboy*, *The Great Escape*, and *Bye Bye Birdie*. That Christmas morning, snowing outside, my father bought me and my sister sleds and we spent the day riding down the rolling countryside. I learned from him then what an ideal father could be. Sometimes I think, what if he had gotten sober, what if he had found someone to bring him into the rooms? I am sure they were there in Peekskill in the early '60s. But that wasn't to be.

MARIJUANA

KIM CONKLIN

Summer brought the Jewish kids from the Riverdale section of the Bronx up for their vacation, a place T. C. Boyle calls "Greasy Lake," a bungalow colony with a long history of left politics hidden away up a long dirt road. Those dudes were always my summer bros. They were way different from my high school friends and every year they came with a surprise. At fifteen it was guitars and folk music and that's where I learned to play, opening my ears to a whole world apart from what I was listening to on AM radio. The next year was chess and the whole summer was about that. But the summer I was to turn seventeen they brought the weed. We had heard about it and knew the freak scene from the Beatles and Stones and the Summer of Love pictured in teen magazines, but I had never gotten high. In my community it was way outside the norm, dangerous, illegal. My city friends could not wait to turn me on. It was in the woods where I got my first taste. "Inhale it, hold it," four of us on that joint but I was not feeling anything. After the third hit I thought, this might not work on me, then bam I was high. I felt it, the release, the cool, the laughter, the drug doing its magical, lethal thing. We walked out of the woods toward a big-ceiling wooden structure called the casino where the parents held meetings and the kids played music at night or hung out when it rained. I think it was the Spoonful's "She Is Still a Mystery" that came floating through the woods. It stopped me. I had been a slave to music my whole life, but I never heard it sound like this.

In college we used to watch a movie called *Reefer Madness* on Friday nights. It was a public service film made in the '30s about the horrors of drug addiction and how the reefer would lead straight to dope, and worse. The whole audience would be laughing at this hysterical film, but I am not laughing anymore because that became my story. From the day that I smoked my first j as a teenager to the day I went into rehab at sixty-one, not a day went by that I didn't get high in one form or another. It's a desire that becomes a lifestyle, then some badge of honor, until everything revolves around it. I use to think it was because of the '60s or because of Keith Richards or William Burroughs but that's all bullshit. Something in me reacts to alcohol and drugs differently than in normal people. You know the feeling when you have had enough, like Thanksgiving after an hour of nonstop eating, when everyone in unison pushes themselves back from the turkey, the stuffing, the wine, the cranberries, the pumpkin pie, and says, "I've had enough." Well I never get that feeling.

Senior year of high school those smart enough to know they weren't going to college had BOCES, some kind of work training program where they went to school in the morning and worked in the afternoon. Kim was in the nursing program. She would show up to school in her father's 1959 green Chevy station wagon, one of the few kids who had permission to drive, always wearing her nurse's outfit. Her father Ernie was Italian so don't ask how he or she got the last name Conklin. Maybe it was her mother's, because that's where she got the long, straight red hair and cute freckles. Slim, athletic, Kimmy carried a giant pocketbook, big enough to keep the ounce of weed she was moving for some mysterious older guy she knew from Ossining, a town further down the Hudson River. In 1969 this was totally outrageous behavior, but I grew up with her and she was the chick who had to climb the highest tree or get us all to go skinny-dipping or whatever. She was a rebel.

Her father was not, he was a primitive gorilla-looking Sicilian, country strong, the boss of the construction company I worked for over the summer.

He ran a crew of mixed-race rough guys, but none of them would give him any problems. Work was laying blacktop, building parking lots and driveways for the locals. I was the teenager in a crew of adults. The blacktop comes off of that truck boiling hot in the already boiling summer afternoon, and you had to move it quick with shovels and rollers and when that shit got on you it burned right through your clothes. Ernie would pick me up every morning at 7 a.m. and I would stand waiting, hungover from the night before, begging my higher power for something to prevent him from coming, but he never failed to turn the corner in that same green station wagon, loaded with enough Dunkin' Donuts and coffee to supercharge a fucking army. Years later I drove by a simple fish fry restaurant out on Route 202 and around the red farmhouse-style building was a parking lot I helped lay one summer day. I felt proud, like I was looking at one of my movies.

It was the jukebox in the coffee shop near the school that played Steppenwolf and the Doors that put the idea in our minds that high school was optional. Up until eleventh grade a yellow bus picked me up at the end of my block and dropped me off at school. Now the get-high seniors would hang out at the cafe before class started, drinking coffee and talking shit, and one morning, while "Magic Carpet Ride" was playing for the third straight time, three plays for a quarter, Kimmy whipped up in that station wagon and off we went, not to school but to someone's apartment in Ossining, her Sodom, to get high and listen to more music. I faked a note from my mother. I didn't plan on Ernie tapping his daughter's phone and hearing who knows what.

I was coming back from school and my father was talking to Ernie out in front of my house, which was strange. I only saw my father cry once, when his mother died. Now, up in my room, I hear him in the bathroom sobbing, talking to himself, saying he has to kill me now.

The opioid epidemic they have now they also had in the '50s in the Bronx. Lucky Luciano and the Italians brought the heroin in thinking they would make a score but keep it to the Puerto Rican and Black neighborhoods. But once you open Pandora's box there's no going back, the shit was out there, and now the young Italians were using it and ODing from it. My second cousin Carmine worked in Jake LaMotta's brother's butcher shop. He was fiercely good-looking, an ass-kicker, a star ballplayer. Everyone in the neighborhood loved him. He let me and my six-year-old crew ride on the handlebars when he made the meat deliveries. I adored him. This part of the Bronx was idyllic but not that idyllic, and they found him dead one morning in the same part of the schoolyard he ruled playing "off the wall." You could hear the screams of the women a block before you got to the funeral parlor, animal moans from his grandmothers. His young mother was comatose. The men stood hard and tough, knowing what was up, but how could they explain it to the rest of us?

Now I hear my father coming down the hall toward my bedroom, still mumbling threats. I never saw him touch my mother or my sisters, no matter how angry he got. He never resorted to getting physical with me either, except for the few times I really put him over the edge, and this was one of them. He would just go for my throat and thank God my mother and sister were there to pull him off. I had to convince him that Kimmy was a liar and was using me as a scapegoat. I swore my innocence. Somehow he believed me.

BUSTED

People ask if I have been to jail and I get very defensive. "Are you crazy, I am a college graduate, an artist." But I have been. The first time was when I was seventeen years old, when an off-duty NYC narcotics officer, long-haired and nasty, pulled his pistol on my friend Ricky while we were parked in front of the cop's house like the idiots we were. I was in the back seat, right behind Ricky, so I had the perfect angle on the gun pointed at his head. The cop asked for the car keys. Ricky proved his delinquency by hesitating before handing them over, while my friend Dicky Shaw and I died a thousand deaths.

We were teenage troublemakers in a Spielberg-type housing development where we didn't live, but we would hang out by the basketball court, the local hot spot that summer. It didn't help that when the younger kids went home we would sit in Ricky's car drinking beer until late. Ricky beat up half the kids in this development, including one of their fathers, so the people in the neighborhood had had enough and, unbeknownst to us, enlisted the off-duty cop, who lived there with a wife and kids, to do something about us.

It was long after the lights went out on the basketball court and everyone had gone to bed. We were sitting in Ricky's mother's big Oldsmobile drinking beer out of cans when the NYC cop came up to our car and told us to get the fuck out of there and never come back. There was a lot of jawing back and forth, but when he threatened to call the police, which in that part of Peekskill is the local state troopers, we left. But Ricky had the bright idea to pull around in front of the cop's house. He said he wanted the exact address so he could report him for threatening us. That idea sounds as ridiculous now as it did then, but he was driving. Ricky was all Irish, with flaming red hair and the attitude that went with it. He was the starting guard on the basketball team and if it wasn't for the fact he was 5' 9" he probably would have played in the pros. He could also fight like Sugar Ray Leonard, so he was a handful. There was no way we were talking him out of it.

As we rolled down the block, trying to figure out where he lived, the experienced street cop stepped out of the bushes and stuck that gun into the side of Ricky's head before we even saw him. I know my father kept a pistol somewhere in the house but I never saw it, much less held it. Now this lethal piece is right in front of my face, and when that hammer got pulled back the sound was heart-stopping. Ricky made the right move, took the keys from the ignition and gave them to him. The cop told us the troopers were on their way, then sat on the lawn and waited, gun out, keys in his hand. Ricky started antagonizing him. "Yo, Deputy Dawg, let's see how tough you are without that gun." Shit like that. The state troopers pulled up. The head sergeant was plenty pissed. He knew us, knew our parents. Ricky cried police brutality when they pulled him out of the car, handcuffed him, and put him in the back of the police car, the sergeant apologizing to the undercover cop for allowing delinquents like us to run loose in his neighborhood. They told me and Dicky to follow them to the station in Ricky's mom's car, where they threw the three of us together in a jail cell and locked it behind us.

Ricky's father owned a construction company and the local radio station, but they couldn't reach him on the phone. After letting us sit awhile, they pulled me out of the cell and told me they needed $150 for bail for Ricky or else we were all sleeping there. I said I needed to ask my father for that kind of money. They said go ahead, but you better come back. It is now past midnight and I am driving Ricky's mother's car, thinking about where I am going to get the nerve to wake up my father and explain everything that had happened. But leave it to my old man, you could never figure this guy out. When I told him, "Ricky had a problem. He needs 150 to get out of jail," he just rolled over in his sleep, opened the tin box he kept in a drawer next to his bed, and handed me the money, saying, "We'll talk about it in the morning."

CALIFORNIA

DRILLER KILLER

ARTHUR WEISBERG

1976 was the worst year of my life. We waited eight months for our porno movie to hit the street, destitute and questioning our film business existence. We were promised a 4th of July opening in the best theater on 42nd Street by Lee Hessel, our distributor, but when that day came it was his other film that was playing. Lee, one of the few non-gangsters we knew in the business, was a Sutton Place gentleman from a distinguished NYC family. His business was bringing sexy European movies into the American marketplace, and he recognized the artistic side of ours. The release finally came in October, not ideal but so what. My poetic title *White Women* was changed to *9 Lives of a Wet Pussy Cat.*

Nicky and I went up to Lee's office after the run was over. In what would become our norm, he told us our film didn't quite "live up to expectations."

"Fine," I said, "where's our money?" He handed us the distribution report. At a coffee shop across the street Nicky and I looked through the paperwork and saw, in black-and-white, the elusive gross, minus the theaters' take, minus the distribution cost, minus the distribution fee, minus, minus, minus. Bottom line is we didn't become instant millionaires. My father never even got his 25k back.

When guys from Peekskill go anywhere they drive. Mac, full name John P. McIntyre, my other lifetime filmmaking partner, had a 914 mid-engine Porsche because he was smart enough to actually have and keep a real job. I was determined to be anywhere but where I was when 1977 rolled in. So on Christmas Eve we took off for LA, leaving my mother and sisters in the driveway holding the presents I bought them, crying and waving goodbye. We hit it Kerouac style, heading south, stopping to see friends in Atlanta and Houston, listening to Robert Johnson and Sonny Boy as the Deep South flew by, then a straight spiritual shot through the West Texas desert to California.

We arrived in Laguna Beach, where our friend Dicky had settled, on New Year's Eve. He took us to a party where the friendliest, coolest people we ever saw welcomed us as if they had known us our whole lives. Soon a really pretty girl comes up to me and says, "You want to go for a swim?" She fired up a lethal joint as she drove me to the beach. I saw the Pacific Ocean for the first time, the sun sinking into it. She pulled off her jeans, saying, “We can’t skinny-dip because the cops’ll bust us,” and jumped into the water in her T-shirt and panties. Someone once told me Keith Richards didn’t wear underwear, so why should I. I went in in just my jeans. I lost track of her in the water and misjudged how far out I was, or how powerful the waves were, or how fucking high I was, and although I have been swimming my whole life I almost drowned there in my welcome to California.

We made it up to Hollywood, unwanted and uninvited. Still, it beat January in NYC. We soon left for San Francisco and there I found what I came for. If you were broke in the ’70s you were better off in San Francisco than New York, and being straight in a seriously gay town opens up other avenues of survival. Menno Meyjes, a schoolmate of mine who would one day write the script for *The Color Purple*, was my guide. He was tall and handsome, originally from Holland, but ended up in Rockland County, in love with a friend of ours, till he broke her heart. A born revolutionary, he was the first one of us to have the courage to head west.

I hadn’t seen him in three years, and when we showed up we were amazed to find him living with an older woman and her five-year-old in a giant space that used to be a firehouse. She had been the wife of one of his professors at the San Francisco Art Institute, so there was the usual drama to go with the domesticity. I would tag along with him to his classes, where I rediscovered my roots, Stan Brakhage and Michael Snow, their surreal abstract films all about the flashing of frames and sound juxtaposition. Plot and character development not a consideration. The Kuchar brothers were also doing crazy out-there shit, more in the John Waters tradition. None of them were sweating grosses or distribution costs.

I had never witnessed a school like the Art Institute. I sat in on classes as if I was enrolled there, no one asking me about tuition. Rosa von Praunheim, a member of the German film wave of Wenders, Fassbinder, and Herzog, was a professor there. He was gay, outrageous. He fucked a porno star on his desk in front of the class, inviting us to film it. That was the curriculum. The next week's class he slaughtered a pig. Thinking about it now it seems like it must have happened on another planet, but it all fit into the vibe of the city at that time. When spring arrived I reluctantly left San Francisco for New York. When you're broke and twenty-six and living on a friend's couch, reality comes calling.

Texas Chainsaw Massacre might have been the most important film in our lives. I saw it at the drive-in theater in Peekskill. By the mid-'70s my once-thriving manufacturing town's factories were empty, the Carvel stand dark and boarded up, the drive-in theater on its last legs, showing slasher films and soft-core porn to cars full of rowdy unemployed locals drinking and drugging. Even the refreshment stand seemed dangerous. This film got their attention. It had a home-brewed dynamic of a semi-documentary nightmare. I mean half of it is a guy in a freak mask chasing a chick around in her underwear screaming her fucking head off, every other shot out of focus. I figured we were capable of matching that. We were laughing our asses off, but by the second weekend there were twice as many people there as week one. Country boys were firing up real chainsaws between the cars. The film grossed something like $35 million on what I heard had been less than a 100k investment. Forget Pasolini, Buñuel, and Godard, Tobe Hooper was our north star. There was an audience for that over-the-top violent stuff that the studios were not yet making, a small window for movies like *Last House on the Left*, *I Spit on Your Grave*, and *Halloween*. My writer Nicky is a genius, and I don't use that term lightly, but you don't need to be one to go from *Texas Chainsaw* to *Driller Killer*. Now I could go to whoever I knew with money with documented proof of a return on a modest investment, that there was a film business that wasn't Triple X. Still my mother was the first money in.

Downtown New York in the summer of 1977 was Son of Sam time. New York Dolls, The Ramones, Basquiat sleeping in the park, abandoned buildings covered in graffiti, violence everywhere. With the power shut off to my apartment for nonpayment I was the last to know about a city-wide blackout that wound up lasting almost three days that summer. My Puerto Rican superintendent Cecelio said, "Now everybody is like you."

Kubrick had just made *Barry Lyndon* and in his desire to shoot a film by candlelight he invented independent cinema. The high-speed Zeiss lenses he adopted, first developed for NASA, along with TVC Labs' new Chemtone process that could further push Kodak's negative, allowed us to shoot NYC at night for the first time. This was revolutionary. Nicky was back teaching school because he knew enough not to count on making movies to earn a living. Mary Kane, my college friend and Mac's girlfriend, gave up her job at a group home in Rockland to become the producer. The plan was to shoot on weekends but not consecutively, do it like the short films we were making in California. I asked David Johansen if he was interested and he looked at me like I was crazy. "You want me to play the Driller Killer?" I ended up playing the role myself because who knew how long this film would take to shoot.

The character was based on our bro, an artist living in his loft near the corner of 18th and Broadway. His real name was Doug Gervasi, changed to Douglas Metro and later Douglas Metrov, billed as Tony Coca-Cola in the movie. I just stepped into his life, a trick we used a bunch of times later on. His band the Roosters were a couple of hot young musicians that Mac brought down from upstate, Ritchie Bittner and a drummer friend, who also had sense enough to keep their day jobs and stay where living was cheap.

Metro was from Ontario, CA. He was a high school wrestling champion, which got him a scholarship to UCLA. He started pre-med but switched almost immediately to the film program, and at some point came to New York to pursue his true gift, which was painting. When I met him he was living uptown, making good money as a commercial artist, but he ditched that to be a serious downtown painter. The giant buffalo, the centerpiece of the film, was commissioned for Union Station in Washington, DC, of all places, to celebrate the Bicentennial. Obviously he was a little late with the delivery. Coming from his university life in Westwood, and the beaches where he hung out and surfed, the filth of the city would get to him. Bums he had a special aversion to and our neighborhood had plenty of them. Eighteenth and Broadway was a haven for old winos and spaced-out Vietnam vets. One night he shared a vision of banging a five-penny nail into the head of the most obnoxious of them with a small sledgehammer. We went with the portable drill. It seemed more elegant.

Metro's stewardess girlfriend Carolyn Marz was one of the leads. She worked for American Airlines and was always generous with her salary and the tiny bottles of liquor she would bring home after a flight. The other female lead was to be Baybi Day, if we could find her. Before the internet you not only got lost, you lost people. Someone's phone number written on a tiny slip of paper drops out of your pocket or you write one digit down wrong and it's goodbye forever. We put the word out we were looking for Baybi, and by pure chance she called one day. When I asked where she had been for a year she told me she was "in Staten Island near a beach." She met a young guy and wound up living in his house with his mother and father. His father was a fisherman with one leg. His son helped him on the boat. I asked her what the fuck did she do out there for so long and she said they would get two half gallons of red wine and the four of them would eat the fish they'd caught and sit around all night watching television. After a year she went out for cigarettes and never came back. Didn't even leave a note. That kid's heartbreak was our good luck.

There was a crazy film rental house with a mix studio called Ross-Gaffney up on 46th Street that specialized in industrials and pornos and under-the-radar commercials. Jim Gaffney presided, gruff and tough with a cigar in his mouth, but he had a big heart he couldn't hide, and he nurtured our ambitions because that was what he was about. *9 Lives* proved to him we were for real, so he made a special deal for us. Whatever equipment hadn't been rented at closing time Friday we could use, as long as it came back in one piece by Monday 7 a.m. So that was the schedule, one weekend at a time, rock till you drop, last man standing kind of shit. Jimmy Lemmo, who went on to do *Ms. 45* with me, was the original DP. We shot four or five weekends during the summer and fall of that year before we ran out of money. With the last of it

I rented a small Steenbeck and somehow got it up to my apartment on 17th and Third with the bathroom down the hall and the bathtub in the kitchen. Now it's the dead of winter and I'm staring at my reflection on the editing table screen, trying to cut together a trailer we can use to sell the movie, freezing, broke, and questioning everything. They say you make plans and God laughs, but God also gives you the spring, and the first hint of it in NYC, the good energy rolling out of the buildings with the people who have been cooped up all winter, was a savior. I had been showing the cut scenes around, and as usual it was 99 percent rejection. But in this business you only need one.

Saul was a Broadway maven with a toupee and a polyester suit. I would meet him in his friend's office that he pretended was his. He was semi-retired, living in Jersey, but couldn't give up the action. His claim to fame was distributing *The Stewardesses* in 3D, which actually made some money. He worked the Triple X stuff but also helped distribute Warhol's films and all kinds of crazy European movies too. He wasn't a guy I needed to explain the business to. He read *Variety* like the Bible. He knew all about *Texas Chainsaw* and he told me maybe Arthur would be interested. Arthur was Arthur Weisberg, a legitimate Jewish gangster from Detroit whose rep was that he once strangled his partner in a car while arguing over a business deal. You off an enemy is one thing, but whacking your own partner, that got our attention.

The first time I spoke to him was on the phone. He had that same gravelly voice as Matty, only a bit more intelligible. He came right out and said he would pay to finish the movie just based on Saul's recommendation. Confirmation, justice, karma, I can't describe the feeling a filmmaker has hearing that he's got the financing. Saul would "move it," his expression for distributing.

Arthur was big-time in the porno game. He was built like Matty too, not as tall, but stocky, muscular, light on his feet like a boxer. Even sitting behind a desk he looked ready to mix it up if he heard one thing he didn't like. He was partners with Mickey Zaffarano, owner of the Pussycat Theaters, a chain of upscale and downscale Triple X houses around the country, the flagship being a stone moneymaker on Broadway.

Mickey was another legitimate tough guy. They had just made *Debbie Does Dallas*, a take-off on the Cowboys cheerleaders, which was grossing $35 million on a $35,000 investment, all in theaters they either owned or controlled. Even *Jaws* couldn't top that profit margin. The studios couldn't legally own theaters so even they had to share their grosses, first with the distributor, then with the sub-distributor, never mind what wound up in the pocketbook of the woman in the ticket booth or those extra large pockets of the theater manager's uniform. Mickey and Arthur didn't have that problem, every dollar coming in was theirs. Nobody working for them would dare touch a nickel.

Contracts were never even discussed. Like Springsteen said about his first contract, "If the guy took off his BVDs, I would have signed those." Weisberg was no fool. Arthur knew about and wanted the seven or eight prints we owned of *9 Lives*, which were gathering dust after Lee Hessel abandoned it. Arthur took those prints and started working them in his theaters all over the Midwest, and that's how we got the 35k to finish *Driller Killer.* We put together a budget and a five-week schedule based on what, who knows. I knew I needed a rock and rollin' DP, a gunslinger, and I found him in Kenny Kelsch.

NYU was the school of De Palma, Scorsese, Jarmusch, the Coen Bros., Spike, and Oliver Stone, but not me. Making *9 Lives of a Wet Pussy Cat* was our graduate school. Like Scorsese, who met Keitel from an ad on a wall in the film department, I taped up a 3x5 file card saying, "Feature film in need of a DP." I got one call.

"I came by the loft, we smoked a couple of joints of cheap Mexican and that was basically the interview" is Kenny's memory of our first meeting. But I remember first meeting him in his small cellar office at NYU. He was a graduate student on the GI Bill wearing a rogue military "Death From Above" T-shirt, long hair, and a nasty attitude. He was one of the guys in charge of handing out equipment and projecting the movies, all the while working on his own feature film. He was born in Jersey City and was studying at a Jesuit seminary when he enlisted in the Army before he could get drafted. He joined the Special Forces and did a tour and a half in Vietnam, and the things he did there as a Green Beret he brought home with him. I once asked him how, trudging through the jungle, they would determine who would walk point. He answered, "I always did. I felt more comfortable there."

Kenny was not interested in seeing the footage we already had because he didn't shoot it, but he read our script. I saw the film he was making and it was good. He had a van, a 16mm camera, and lighting equipment, plus two evil Dobermans to protect the shit. Dale, his beautiful girlfriend, was one of the best assistant camera people we ever had. We all lived and shot in the building on 18th Street. Jimmy the Potter gave us the front of his loft on the seventh floor as an editing space. The fourth floor was vacant altogether, so we got that for nothing. We were using half a building on 5th Avenue for less than $500 a month.

We shoot fast now, but we didn't then. We still had a lot to learn. We kept the exteriors as close to home as possible so we could plug lights into the wall sockets and point them out onto the street from the fourth-floor window. When we had to leave our block Mac or Kenny would tie into the street lights for power. You had to be on the lookout, or shoot late at night, because the cops didn't put up with that shit. One rainy Friday at magic hour Kenny was working his voltage tester with the little bulb on the back that tells you what's hot, and I watched him blow out every traffic light along Broadway from Union Square to 23rd Street.

Ms. 45

Driller Killer opened in Kansas City on a summer weekend in 1979 and was far and away the best box office performance we ever had. The city of Jean Harlow, Charlie Parker, and Marla Hanson ate it up. Playing in a few slasher houses and a bunch of drive-ins, the film smoked the Hollywood competition. It was far from the $25 million of *Texas Chainsaw*, but it was enough. I got an immediate call from Arthur, who started off screaming, "You think you're a fucking big shot now? You guys ain't shit. What are you doing next?" When you're doing business that's how quick it is to get your next picture. I had what I wanted to do, a cool script Nicky had just written that we were calling *Ms. 45*.

With Nick the shit would just arrive by mail. We never talked about what he was working on because we considered it bad luck. I opened the envelope, sat down, and read the exact movie that ended up in the theater. Like *The Addiction* or *The Funeral* afterward, there was no rewriting and not a lot of questions to ask. It was clear, concise, and dynamite. I gave Arthur the opening, which was a young seamstress gets raped on her way home from work, and when she gets back to her apartment a guy who's there robbing the place rapes her again. Arthur wanted to know the title, and when I told him *Ms. 45* he gave me the money. Easy as that. 7k a week for eight weeks, and a NYC lab to supply the film stock, the developing, and the post work.

Performance, Pink Flamingos, El Topo were the midnight movies, the new thing happening at the time. *The Driller Killer* was screened for a guy who could have distributed it that way after it had its pretty decent slasher run. I was in the other room listening through a closed door when the distributor told Saul that the film did not look or sound professional enough to be considered. I should have laughed and gone home, because seeing it now that film looks and sounds just like it's supposed to. But at the time I took it to heart. I was crushed. It was our second feature and I did not have the self-esteem to trust myself or our work. Instead I wanted what was on those marquees I walked under on my way home. A real fucking movie, 35mm for def, shot with a professional crew on Panaflex equipment. For the first time, but not the last, I walked away from the key crew members who helped me get to this point. Why didn't I just keep the faith in what we had, a loft in downtown Manhattan, a group of filmmaking friends, low-budget shit that was working? Let the world come to us, like the Wooster Group in their garage downtown. Was it the idea that something bigger was out there? The Buddhists call it attachment, which also means desire, expectation. It leads nowhere. But don't tell that to an American kid still twenty-five years from his first Buddhist teaching. Kenny once said it was all downhill after *Driller Killer*. He might have been right.

NYC style comes from three guys, the holy trinity. Owen Roizman, who besides *French Connection* shot *The Exorcist*, Gordon Willis, who shot *Godfather* and *Manhattan*, and Michael Chapman, who shot *Raging Bull*. There was the bar, clear as day and high as hell. I brought back Jimmy Lemmo, who was now the 2nd assistant cameraman for Roizman, to be the DP, and he brought some of his guys from that crew. It was basically an IA union team working above their positions. They all changed their names to protect their union status. We kept it as low-key as possible, but Jimmy still got a cement block tossed through the passenger-side window of his BMW. At least they waited for the car to be parked. His cousin Sal worked at Panavision, and he somehow managed to get us the 35mm Gold model. Godard says the camera itself sets the tone for the whole film, so pick your box with care. For the IA guys this was nothing special, but my crew and I stared at that camera and touched it like it could disappear at any moment.

Arthur was making high-grossing Triple X films in five days using a third of the film stock I needed for *Ms. 45.* In their world everything you shoot ends up in the movie, so seeing the amount of film we were using and our lengthy shooting schedule he was convinced we were using his money to make a second movie on the side. I would get a call from him at some crazy hour, telling me in his low growl that if I was making another movie behind his back he would kill me. That's the kind of people I was in business with.

UNCLE BOBO

My uncle Bobo was a dreamer. My other uncles and my father were hustlers. Money was the singular goal and work was a nonstop activity. Outright thieving was a no-no. In my particular tribe, it was the lowest thing you could do, and being called a thief was the ultimate insult. My eight-year-old cousin Anthony couldn't help himself. I was always tagging along behind him, so I was right there when his father dragged him screaming back through the neighborhood to return the few packs of baseball cards he had lifted from the local candy store. The owner acted like it was no big deal. It was a big deal to my uncle Tom.

Uncle Bobo was the baby of the family, a thin, good-looking Italian dude, a shorter version of Dean Martin. Unlike his brothers, working was not a top priority. He connected with his nephews on a level few adults could. He was always there for me, in ways my father didn't have the time or understanding to be. When I was a kid we played in the street, every NYC game with a pink rubber ball, slap, off the stoop, stickball. It would be well after 12 noon when my uncle would make his appearance, emerging onto the second-floor balcony dressed immaculately, suit and tie, white-on-white shirt, cuff links, greased up and smelling good, a hot summer day but he's not sweating, he's cool. From up above he would pick one of his nephews to go with him on his daily rounds. You would hear "Dominic" or "Anthony" or "Brother," which was my nickname. We needed nicknames because all of the first sons were named Abel, after my grandfather. I thought I had a very common name until I went out in the world and didn't meet another Abel till I was thirty years old. Why Bobo needed a seven-year-old to keep him company was unknown. He would come down the steps handing out copious amounts of change to us kids, nephews or not. I would get in his Caddy and lean back as we rolled through the streets. He was hitting every bar they were doing business with, delivering contraband cigarettes, picking up money from the jukeboxes and cigarette machines, and collecting or paying out money from the bookmaking. Baseball, numbers, and horse racing, the three deities.

The bars in the early afternoon were dark and empty. My uncle would sit with the owner, who would pour me a giant syrupy coke from the tap and throw in a bunch of maraschino cherries. With endless coins from the register, the shuffleboard table and the jukebox were mine. I would play Jack Scott's "Leroy" over and over, till I pushed the guy over the edge and he told my uncle I had to cut that out. Then it was "Bird Dog" by the Everly Brothers. My uncle didn't mind. As long as I was happy he was cool.

Confirmation Sunday is your Catholic bar mitzvah, a coming-of-age moment in our church. Even in Peekskill, where the church was a low, modern '60s-style building, it was a big deal. What was a bigger deal was that I was pitching for my Little League team against the first-place Apaches that afternoon after the church service. In suburban America Little League was more of a ritual than church. In fact the well-kept fenced-in field was right behind the church, with bleachers on the first and third base sides, and even an announcer, someone's mother, talking through a loudspeaker.

It was a hot day in June and I was all dressed in my confirmation suit, waiting for my uncle. It was worth the wait. He pulled up in a new two-tone mahogany Caddy, wearing a beautiful coppery iridescent suit with black stitching that matched the car. A lifetime later I was able to explain the suit to the tailor on Fifth Avenue and 19th Street, who made three to order for Nicky, Mac, and me for the day I got married.

My uncle took something wrapped in simple paper from his jacket pocket and handed it to me. A gold watch. A watch was the go-to confirmation gift, all the boys in their robes were wearing them, but most were sorry Timexes with leather straps, nothing like the piece he gave me. Then he reached back in the car and took out something else, his new Bell & Howell 8mm camera. "It's to make home movies," he said. I had seen them around, and we had them at school, but my uncle was the only person in my extended family to think of buying one.

Bobo did not care much for baseball, even though gambling was our family business. He threw like a girl. In a family where one of my other uncles played semipro ball, where Joe DiMaggio was God and Frank Malzone, the great third baseman for the Boston Red Sox, lived down the street, this was odd. But he was the one who took me to my first ball game. The Grand Concourse and 161st Street was not far from where I lived, but entering Yankee Stadium was otherworldly. We got there in the middle of the game because my uncle only came for some in-person bookmaking and could care less about watching it. It was daytime, in the middle of the week, so there was not a big crowd. The grass was so green that coming up the ramp was like entering an emerald city and right in front of me, kneeling in the batter's box, was Mickey Mantle. Marvel superheroes don't come close. Ballplayers weren't physically big back then, but he was. The number 7 stretching across his massive back, he looked with nonchalance at the pitcher he was about to face, knowing there was nothing he had that he couldn't hit. And when Mickey hit them out they would go so high that the crowd stood and watched for what felt like forever, lingering in ecstasy.

Abbot Morris was bar mitzvah'd, not confirmed, and he didn't go to our school, so we only saw him at the Little League games when we played his team. Anyone who thinks Jewish dudes can't play ball never saw him hit. He was left-handed and built big like a young Babe Ruth. He would pick the biggest bat available, the one the rest of us could barely lift, and twirl it around like a magic wand. He stood in a wide-open stance, facing the mound, daring you to even throw the ball. I was only eleven, but I was the starting pitcher for my underdog team. I got him out the first time he was up. He hit a bullet to right field, which is where you stick your worst player, and our right fielder Robert qualified. Robert didn't have time to do anything but catch it or get killed by it. Thankfully it buried in his glove and stayed there.

His second time up Abbot wanted revenge. It was the fourth inning and we were miraculously ahead by a run, but they had guys on base. The sun was pounding down and my manager was screaming the usual at me, "Take your time, bear down!" My father, standing behind the batting cage, where he always stood when I pitched, shouted instructions at my best friend

Chucky, my catcher. Chucky had an abusive father so he was taking it all in stride. I looked to the stands and my uncle was calmly filming it all, oblivious to the score or the drama of the moment, just happy that his nephew was center stage. Abbot Morris was looking at me with such a dismissive attitude I wished I had a 90-mile-an-hour fastball to throw right in his face. I took my time, bore down, and delivered. Abbot hit the ball so far it shocked everyone. Robert, with his black eyeglasses all masking-taped together, never moved an inch. He just turned and watched in wonder with the rest of us. Abbot was almost to second base by the time the ball landed. I turned away from this almost thirteen-year-old, laughing at me as he jogged around the bases, to see my manager and my father holding their heads in disgust. I wanted to take that beautiful uniform off right there and go home to my mother.

The crowd was booing and begging my manager to get me out of there, which was the right move. Then I heard a different kind of commotion coming from the third base bleachers. There was a fight in the stands, an actual fight between adults, which had never happened before. My uncle Bobo was in a fistfight with one of my teammate's fathers. People were screaming. I watched in disbelief. My father raced into the stands to break it up. "What's wrong with you?" he screamed at my poor uncle in front of everybody. My uncle's defense was, "He kept calling Abel a bum."

The ride home was a disaster. No one can get pissed

off like my old man, and between the realization that his son would never be a Major League baseball player and his younger brother would always be a hopeless sociopath, he was on fire. Once these kind of Italians get worked up there is no stopping them. My uncle sat there quietly, knowing he had disappointed his older brother, the most important person in his life, again. But as we got out of the car, and my father's back was turned, he shot me the goofiest child's face as if to say, it's all right, in our world everything is ok.

My aunt Ruthie, Bobo's wife, had the intelligence and exotic beauty of Bess Myerson, the first Jewish Miss America and later a NYC commissioner, also from the Bronx. My aunt fell hard at sixteen for my slick little wop uncle who was twenty-one at the time. Her father Murray disowned her when he found out she was pregnant and about to marry a gentile. Her own mother had to sneak behind Murray's back to go see her. It was my father who finally turned the guy around. He went into Murray's furrier shop and, in front of his workers, presented him with his own grandchild.

Bobo and his wife Ruthie lost four children, either during pregnancy or in the first year of their lives. It was due to an Rh factor in their blood. I was too young to have it explained to me. My uncle brought me with him to our empty church in the middle of the afternoon and I knelt beside him, watching him cry. They had one beautiful daughter who survived, and later on they adopted a son.

My aunt's love for my uncle lasted till the day he died and beyond. But the real world was too much for him, all those Bronx rules, siege mentality, tough guys win. He lived another way, that dreaming was as valid as real life. He had depression issues, which his alcoholism made worse. Seeing a psychiatrist or god forbid going into recovery was completely alien to my family. But my aunt was smart and resourceful, and eventually got him into a high-priced rehab in Connecticut where he shared a room with Truman Capote. He was not good with names so it took me forever to understand who he was talking about. "You know, that guy on TV that talks with that high lispy voice, you know that little fairy who is always on the TV."

I came home that Christmas and my father was in a funk. He said, "How can we have Christmas when your uncle's in that place?" The fact is we should have been celebrating. Finally, in a family of alcoholics, someone was getting the help they needed. But my father didn't know any better and I didn't either. I was in my late twenties and I should have been in that hospital right next to him and Truman. Truman never got sober, and I had a long, bad way to go. My uncle never drank again.

CAT CHASER

ELMORE LEONARD

Elmore Leonard is like no other writer. Someone called him the Mark Twain of the twentieth century. He weaves the spell. *Cat Chaser* was my introduction to him. The book is deceptively simple, easy to read, impossible to put down. It's set in the cocaine-fueled Miami of the 1980s. The backstory is the American invasion of the Dominican Republic in 1964, a street war used as a warm-up for Vietnam. A young marine named Moran is taken prisoner by a beautiful young Dominican guerrilla named Luci Palma. When it comes to the interrogation her only question to him is, "Who do you like better, the Beatles or the Rolling Stones?" The villain, an evil ex-NYC detective named Jiggs Scully, is one of Elmore's greatest creations.

The script was mind-numbingly awful. Not one word of Elmore's brilliant dialogue survived, replaced by some shit one of the producers and his Hollywood hack co-writer found cute or funny. I read it on the plane and I should have left it in the seat pocket in front of me and got on the next flight back to New York. But I didn't, the movie was already a go, and besides I have the kind of ego that tells me just give me a budget and the actors and I can make it work. Wrong.

The first meeting was with Peter Davis, the shark side of the Davis-Panzer production team who was producing the film. Peter, being from New York, laid down the law in terms I could understand. "We hear you're some kind of hotshot producer, and you want to bring your woman co-producer out here with you. Well, we're not interested. You're being hired to be a director, got it? You do the directing, I do the producing, and you can leave your friends at home. The budget is six million, you're getting 350,000, and how the rest of it gets spent is none of your fucking business." All I heard was the 350, which was way more than I had ever thought about getting paid. I said ok, and that was the end of that meeting.

His partner Bill Panzer was a Baby Huey–looking dude, very tall and very alcoholic. Even as a budding one myself, I thought this guy really has a problem. He fancied himself an intellectual, a creative genius, and it turned out he coauthored the nightmare they considered the final draft of the script. I met him at "his place in NYC," a cool downtown loft overlooking the river on the West Side. He was pulling groceries out of a bag, preparing a gourmet lunch, all very homey stuff, pouring vodka shots as he was opening the wine he was gonna serve. The occasion was to meet Peter Weller, who had just done *Robocop*, and was key to green-lighting the film. The pre-game speech was, "Peter has many offers he is considering and we need to convince him he needs to do ours first." As the doorbell rang Bill whispered, "Whatever you do, don't discuss the script. He told his agents he loved it. Now is not the time to bring up your reservations."

Peter is cool and smart. He knew Elmore Leonard personally. We talked casting choices and start dates and it all seemed promising. When Bill went back to the kitchen to check on the cooking, Peter told me up front he couldn't stand the script. We agreed on the spot we would go for the novel all the way, a page one rewrite based on Elmore's book. We headed to the kitchen to confront Bill and found him on the phone, asking a rental agent for half the day rate back on the apartment that was supposedly his. Never mind the dude lying to us about how much we both loved his script, he was lying about the apartment we were standing in.

Bill actually made us a delicious lunch, and I still remember the white wine, crisp, cold, and expensive, and Bill and I drinking way more than a bottle. Peter didn't have any. He was already sober, and a Buddhist to boot, so the solution was right in front of me.

My daughter Endira was still a baby. Her younger sister Lucy wasn't even born yet. Their childhoods were ruined by my drinking and drugging. You can't live in regret, but how do you not regret that? I was miles away from understanding "one day at a time," or the Buddha, "one breath at a time." Practicing those concepts has made a serious difference in the quality of my life. Even Elmore learned from the program. He said, "It taught me how to listen."

"Elmore is in town and we're going to meet him this afternoon," Panzer told me early one Sunday morning. "See if you can move to the best room in the hotel for a couple hours."

"Yeah, no problem." I was on their payroll now, and part of the Davis-Panzer style of operation. The hotel was the Marmont. They arrived at three, Panzer and Davis dressed strangely in tennis whites. They never played tennis in their lives, but that's how they wanted to be perceived. Bill even had a racquet. Weller arrived looking like the movie star he is, and Elmore was dressed like a high school teacher from Michigan, sports jacket with elbow patches and a tie. Only this was no high school teacher, this was the real McCoy, a guy who cut his teeth on dime novels and B movie scripts and went on to become one of the great American novelists.

The beauty of the book is that Moran, the ex-marine, doesn't wear his toughness on his sleeve. He gets himself out of dangerous situations by exploiting the flaws he detects in others. Leonard waits until the final scene to play the ultra-violence card, Moran shooting Jiggs Scully point-blank with his military-issue .45, dealing with life on his own terms and laying down the law of his own personal justice. That scene came too late for Weller. He needed it sooner, and the other two wanted all the action they could get. I would go off in a situation like that and start demeaning and bullying anyone daring to suggest changes to my story. But Elmore reacted like the Dalai Lama, calmly weighing their concerns and resolving them right before our eyes, putting together plotlines like some savant, a magician pulling cards out of thin air. The meeting ended and I sat there with my mind blown. The other three, who insisted on calling him "Dutch," left happy, convinced they were finally getting their money's worth for the book rights. Alone, I had to ask him, "How do you put up with this?" He said, "I'm writing a book about Hollywood and I'm here to research it. I'll be on the first train out of Dodge tomorrow." As I walked him to the door he graciously invited me to dinner. Then he added, "Tell me one thing, which one was Panzer and which one was Davis?"

Dinner was at Chianti, a classic Italian place on Melrose. Sitting in a booth with him was the payoff for all the bullshit this film was going to put me through. The book he was researching was *Get Shorty*, but he wanted to talk about the one he was currently writing. It opened with a Detroit wise guy who would do his business in Toronto only when the Tigers played the Blue Jays there. It was his little vacation ritual, go to the stadium, have a trusted call girl up to his hotel suite, a bottle of Dom Pérignon sent up, do his thing, and next morning fly back to Detroit. Well this time the call girl wasn't so trusted. She was told, "When he calls for the champagne, tell him you'd like to take a shower first and just wait under the water." The room service waiter came, opened the bottle of champagne, and while the guy was tasting it, blasted him. Then he walked into the bathroom, opened the shower curtain, and blasted her too. Elmore's openings were as good as his endings.

I wound up in *Get Shorty*. Elmore wrote, "Nobody wore a necktie. They'd wear a suit and leave the shirt open. Or the thing now, they'd button the shirt collar, wearing it with a suit but no tie, like they were getting away with something. Instead they looked like they'd just come off the fucking reservation."

GRANDFATHER

MY FATHER 2

My grandfather was from a town called Sarno in the south of Italy between Salerno and Napoli. Abele is the Italian spelling. He was named after the second son, Cain's brother, the first victim of God's world. He was a man of the land but he could read and write. It was 1900 when he had enough of picking tomatoes in 100 degree heat. He had heard enough stories from people who had traveled to America to know there was something there for him, and one day he just started walking. Sarno is a long way on foot from Napoli, but that's how he got there. Italians are like that anyway, a lot of Christopher Columbus in them. Naples was another planet to a nineteen-year-old from the countryside. It was called the Paris of southern Europe, with its street life and theaters and the beginnings of the Italian cinema surrounding him. He had cousins there and after a couple of weeks they got him on a ship to New York, not riding third class but no class. He was a stowaway.

He arrived at Ellis Island. I think of the reception you would get at Kennedy Airport today if you showed up with no passport and no ticket and no money, just a cousin's name and a street address on the Lower East Side. But what he got was opportunity, Germans and Irishmen waiting for WOPS (With Out Papers) to hand them a pick and shovel to help build the Lexington Avenue subway or the cross-country railroad. He found his cousin, who had a school in Little Italy teaching new arrivals to read and write English, how to act less greaseball and more American. I would have loved to have filmed those classes. My grandfather was an honest hardworking guy, but slave labor wasn't his thing. He could've stayed in Southern Italy for that. After six months and a few classes he went from laying the tracks to riding them, somehow making it to northern California. He got involved in a deal to buy grapes and came back to NYC with a boxcar full of them to sell to his wine-starved countrymen. He did this a couple of times and made enough money so that when he returned to Sarno he was riding in a ship's cabin.

He rolled into his hometown on a train with a pocketful of money and stood in the town square talking up the USA like it was heaven on earth, offering to front the cost to anyone that wanted to go back with him. My grandmother's response was "What took you so long?" That was the kind of chick she was, tough, not big on smiles. They got married and a whole gang of them headed back to America. His brother lasted a month before realizing he couldn't stand the place and went home for good. My grandmother was no big fan either, but she got so seasick on the ride over she wasn't taking that trip ever again. She lived the rest of her life in the Bronx. She got my grandfather to move out of the South Bronx and up to the Morris Park section, which back then looked exactly like the countryside they had left. There they re-created the traditional culture of their compagna. My father and my uncles and my aunts, eight of them after three died, were all born there, but none of them spoke a word of English till they started going to school.

My grandmother sold miracles. Her house was full of pictures and statues of saints. Neighborhood women would come in and paste dollar bills on them with specific requests. My grandmother kept track of which ones did what and which prayers were necessary and took a commission. I would come home to statues flying out the window when they didn't come through. It was personal.

It was a Sunday afternoon in the Bronx. I was in the seat next to my father, my mother beehived and beautiful in the back with my sister. Amerigo's was a fancy place with waiters in bow ties and the maître d' in a tux, as old-school as it gets. It was the meeting place every Sunday for my father and his business associates, where they could show off their families and teach us how to behave in a restaurant. We pulled into a parking space across the street, diagonally between two cars. There were two dudes on the sidewalk, both looking like the Fonz, only this was the mid-'50s in the Bronx and these were real delinquents. They approached my father, who had just gotten out of the car and closed his door. One said, "You can't park here, this is our space." My father just looked at him. Nothing pissed off my old man more than an Elvis haircut, unless it was a leather jacket with zippers. The kid repeated, "You didn't hear me, get this car out of here." My mother, knowing her husband, rolled down her window. "Al, let's just go." The dude leaned over, saying, "Shut this bitch up," but he never got to the last word. My old man grabbed him by the neck and slammed his face into the driver's-side window. The flash of shock and agony and blood on the kid's face through the spidering glass before he slid to the ground has lasted with me this long. So has the sound of my mother and sister screaming. The other dude had sense enough to run, my father, in his suit and tie and cashmere overcoat, now in primal mode. From across the street the maître d' and a waiter ran toward us, calling Al! Al! Seeing the kid out cold on the ground they figured the fight was over. But my father was just warming up. He dragged the kid to the front of the car and pushed his head under the front tire, demanding that the waiter get in and drive over the dude while the rest of us sat inside. The maître d' managed to calm my father down and walked us all across the street, where we sat at our usual table and had lunch. Normal people would have discussed the incident forever. Not us. My mother, my sister, and I never brought it up. I'm sure my father forgot it even happened. I didn't love him any less for it, it was just who he was, and I always had to keep that in mind.

My father, unlike his brothers, wasn't short or skinny. He was close to six feet, and when they say country strong, he was city strong. He was born in the South Bronx and the difference between Morris Park Ave, where I grew up, and Morris Ave was the difference between heaven and hell. The ghetto is the ghetto, whether Italian, Black, Puerto Rican, or now West African. He grew up fighting and shooting. Some serious gangsters came from the Bronx, Dutch Schultz, Mad Dog Coll, O. G. Mack, the list is long and illustrious. My father grew up as the Roaring '20s flipped into the Depression, so his ambition was born of desperation. He was thirteen years old when his father had a nervous breakdown after losing all the property he owned to the real estate sharks. My grandfather couldn't speak English, couldn't defend himself, so thirty years of hard work was ripped off of him using the stock market crash as an excuse. He split back to Italy, to his mother, to put his mind back together. My father and his older brothers had to leave school to feed the family. He told me how they would go into the hospital where my grandmother was giving birth to yet another kid and dump the money on the hospital bed, money he made selling newspapers on the corner, hustling scrap metal and old rags, or shooting dice, which was one of my old man's specialties. At his funeral one of his best friends came up to console me, saying, "Your father was the best crapshooter I ever met."

By twenty-one my father was a bar owner and a bookmaker, and connected, because in that neighborhood you're born connected. He spoke their language, the Neapolitan dialect. My grandfather was a simple, honest, hardworking guy with no criminal intent. My father kept the hardworking part and added the criminality. He owned a Chinese restaurant in the Bronx called the Burma Bar, catering to a Jewish clientele. At night it turned into a cabaret with comedians, a floor show, and a big band. Down the street was Jake LaMotta's place, "a real sawdust joint" according to my uncle Bobo. The entertainment there was a makeshift ring in the back room where alcohol-fueled tough guys would get a chance to win 50 bucks if they could knock Jake down. I imagine them fighting in their white shirts and suit pants, Jake beating the shit out of them.

Bobo was a young Casanova, but when he brought a sixteen-year-old local beauty called Vicky into my father's place my father told him to get her out of there before they lost their liquor license. So he brought her down to Jake's, where I guess there was no age limit. My uncle had no interest in seeing *Raging Bull*, never mind reading the book. He was shocked they made a movie about Jake or anyone from that hood. For him movie characters were reserved for heroes like Ben-Hur or Wyatt Earp. He would look around to make sure my mother or aunt was not in earshot. "You know what he would do, you know what Jake would do? He would pimp out his own wife."

De Niro and Scorsese got this world letter-perfect, and so did Mike Tyson in his book about growing up with his stepfather Cus D'Amato, written with Ratso Sloman. I empathized with his experience, growing up with a madman you loved because he was capable of loving you back. Cus was one of my father's best friends growing up. My uncle would rhapsodize about late nights keeping him company at the gas station where he worked, acting as backup in case someone tried to rip it off. Cus would talk of the moon and the stars and the mysteries of the universe in a neighborhood where no one saw above the rooftops.

My uncle always told me, "If we had only stayed in the Bronx, none of this would have happened." But my father needed the big lights, he needed Manhattan, he needed to prove himself with the real serious players. Mulberry Street is where he hooked up with a racketeer they called Sally Burns. Who knows what his real name was, but he was the real deal. My father became Sally's junior partner. He moved from his local neighborhood business to owning after-hours clubs in downtown Manhattan and a bar in Miami Beach, with trips to Havana with his new crew. It was all *Godfather II* shit until his addiction kicked in.

It was the spring of 1980 and I was putting the finishing touches on *Ms. 45* when my father finished the job with another alcohol and pill overdose. A year earlier he was doing well, with a straight reputation in Peekskill, good friends, and enough money to last a normal person a lifetime. But that wasn't enough for him. Maybe he missed Sunday dinners with the extended family at my grandmother's, surrounded by thirty people with the same last name, or maybe it was my sisters and I disappearing into our own lives that pushed him further into a fragile place.

He spent the last week of his life in a coma in a local hospital. My sister said over the phone, "Daddy didn't make it." I don't know what I felt. I went down to the '67 Mustang that she had leant me, parked out in front of the loft. With four on the floor and a Hurst shift I barreled up the West Side Highway back home, the Hudson River at night keeping me company and a million thoughts racing through my mind.

My mother was alone, sitting in the dark in my father's chair in the basement, composed and quiet.

She told me how it happened. A week earlier he went into his bedroom, downed a vial of Percodans and chased it with a bottle of Seagram's 7. He went into the kitchen and heated up some soup. Five minutes later he tumbled down the stairs, landing at her feet. "Give me a minute, I will be ok," he told her, the last words of a fighter waiting for the final bell, which rang for him that night.

For the first time, she told me the story of his first try at suicide when I was a kid. If his partner hadn't forgotten his keys, I thought, I would have grown up without a father.

In the end the guy hung in there for us, he never left his family or allowed it to break up, which is more than I can say for myself. For those living daily with him it was like Hurricane Katrina finally blew out to sea. It was tough for me to see the people who loved him most relieved to see him gone. I resented my mother and sisters and his two sisters for that. You couldn't blame them, but I did. I had been out of the house since I was seventeen and had kept enough distance to maintain the romantic ideal of him, a legitimate tough guy who put it all on the nose time and again, who never backed down from anything or anyone. For a guy who generated millions of dollars in his life, all he left was a cashier's check for $1,500, stuck on a clip on his desk like a flag waving, a last offering to my mother and sisters and me. There was a period I used to celebrate his birthday by popping a

Percodan with a glass of Seagram's 7 and just a splash of water. It would knock the shit out of me. It's hard to imagine he'd start with Seagram's in the morning instead of coffee and go on all day from there, popping those pills like candy.

He would always say what little success he saw us have was thanks to the money he never got back on *9 Lives.* He would guilt us, saying we were too busy carousing, chasing girls and acting like movie stars, when we should have been concentrating on collecting his money. I would hear it whenever I came back from an LA trip. He would get up from his recliner down in his playroom with the full-length working bar and the ball game on TV, put his arms around me, and hug me so that every bone in my body was cracking. Then he would stare into my eyes like a homicide detective, slap me across the face with an affection that rattled my brain, give me the biggest, wettest kiss you ever got, and call up to my mother, "Hey, Mr. Big is back from Hollywood."

On the first night of his wake his close friend Lindy, who had made a fortune in the plumbing supply business, pulled a folded-up document from his pocket, stating that he had made a 20k investment into *9 Lives.* This was news to me. He said, "Your father told me if anything happened to him you would make good on this." That was also news to me, because my father beat into my head that if anything happened to him I didn't owe anyone anything. But by the end of the night four more of his friends had approached me with the same story and their own pieces of paper. It turned out my father had actually raised 75k for the film, giving us 25 and keeping 50 for himself, and guilting the shit out of us for the rest of his life. His final lesson.

DINO

KING OF NEW YORK

Dino De Laurentiis was one of maybe five people who could single-handedly green-light a movie, but only he could make it happen in an instant. His office was in the Gulf & Western building, the same building Paramount was in. Sometimes I would get a call at like 6 a.m., Dino himself on the phone saying, "Come up here, I need to talk to you." He was working European hours, and when I got there he would be the only person in the building, on the phone doing his Italian business. That morning he showed me a stack of scripts four feet high that he had commissioned for *Year of the Dragon.* He wanted me to show them to Nicky to see if we could mix and match all these attempts into one good one. *Year of the Dragon* was his *Star Wars,* his vision for a film that would unite East and West into one mass movement to the box office. It would be about the two gangs in New York's Chinatown, the Ghost Shadows and the Flying Dragons, bitter enemies. I knew all about them, and stayed miles away. Machine-gunning up local restaurants was their MO, they could care less about tourists or whoever else. The Italians did not have a monopoly on unchecked violence in the early '80s.

I had no interest in his idea because we were working on our own called *Murder One.* It was inspired directly by *The Terminator.* I saw it on a Saturday night at a theater in the West Village near 8th Street that had the feel of a 42nd Street house. The theater was packed, racially mixed, everyone talking at the screen, stoned out and blown away by what they were looking at. Dino would explain later, "Schwarz-a-neggar is a-playin' the badda guy." There was more to it than that. Cameron knows what the audience is looking for and how to give it to them. I was getting the same hit that George Miller delivered in *The Road Warrior,* a physical rush. I wanted to do that too. I walked up Seventh Ave, took a right at 18th Street, went straight up to my loft and started pounding out a scene. It began with shooting up a church funeral and ended with the shooter disguised as a Hassid getting the jump on his pursuers and murdering all of them. I called him Jimmy Jump. It was only a start, but it was the vibe that I passed on to Nicky. We eventually called it *King of New York.*

We made a meeting with Dino, who would hear our pitch if we came to see him in North Carolina.

He wanted to show us the new studio he had built to shoot *Year of the Dragon* after he'd been thrown out of Chinatown, the neighborhood protesting him filming what was actually going on down there. We arrived and they gave us a golf cart to drive around what was a pretty close facsimile to Cinecittà Studios, complete with a fully stocked Italian deli, all thrown up there in the middle of Appalachia. The Italian craftsmen he brought over, mixed with cheap local help, built an incredible replica of Mott Street.

The meeting with Dino was in Italian, because Nicky could speak it and Dino's English was sketchy. Every conversation takes twice as long in Italian, so I read the body language as Nicky pleaded the case for *King of New York.* We stayed the night at Dino's new hotel while he supposedly read the script. The verdict came the next morning, in English: "Me no like."

A while back Dino had built a state-of-the-art giant water tank in Tunisia somewhere for *Orca,* his whale movie. He was obsessed that this pool was just sitting in the desert collecting dust, so somewhere in every meeting we would hear his plea to find something to do there. To come all the way here for a meeting with Dino and go home empty-handed to our group and our families was the pits. The runway was in full view of his office and the plane we were going back to New York on was revving up. Somewhere between an existing set needing a story and god knows what, I blurted out, "What about a movie about an Italian boy from Little Italy who falls in love with a Chinese girl, Romeo and Juliet, modern, violent, and we can shoot it here." Even Nicky wasn't expecting that. He repeated it to Dino in Italian. Dino said yes and we had a deal.

Year of the Dragon with Cimino and Mickey Rourke was a colossal disaster. *China Girl*, which we made with Vestron and not De Laurentiis, on the streets of Little Italy and Chinatown and not in North Carolina, did worse, if that was possible. Dino miscalculated. No one was interested in Chinese gangs, not even the Chinese.

King of New York, unlike our other scripts, took time as we honed the scenes and point of view, moving from a cop movie to a film about a gangster. We called him Frank after Henry Fonda in *Once Upon a Time in the West*, and where White came from who knows. Biggie was checked into his hotel as Frank White on the night he was killed. Movies have a strange effect on people. It was a lot of Joey Gallo stuff, but we were going for icon logic, not real gangster shit.

My lawyer Jay Julien was working with our European agent Vittorio Squillante, who was one of the few guys over there who could speak English. Augusto Caminito, a client of his, was hooked up with Silvio Berlusconi and Mario Cecchi Gori. They were loaded with cash and were looking for things American, Pacino or De Niro number one, but any actor from that ilk, and because I had an Italian last name it was all the better. In this business you cannot question the source of the financing, you will never get anywhere. You can console yourself by saying that by making a film you are morally cleansing the capital and changing it into something for the good. Whatever the rationale I never turned down a penny from an investor, whether it came from drug dealing or gun running or anywhere else.

We didn't know Walken at the time, but Jay represented him and gave him the script. He liked it. A meeting was set up at my apartment on Perry Street, and while Nicky and I were waiting we tried out all the things we would say to him and little strategies we might use to coerce him into the film. He showed up as advertised, tall, elegant, mysterious, and like every time I would ever meet with him he just appeared, alone, carrying a black bag like a doctor. We all sat quiet for a moment. I had no idea where to begin. He started talking. He said you can't play a king, it's the attitude of the other actors toward you that makes you one. Then he stood up and said, "I read the script and I know exactly what you guys want, and I can give it to you." We couldn't even manage a response. He said he had to go and left, never having taken off his coat. I went right to the phone to call Jay to try to figure out what just happened. He said, "Well, I guess you have your actor."

With Walken locked in Jay and I flew to Rome to meet the money guys in person. We were taken to a villa outside of the city. We had lunch with some of them and might have even shook hands with Mario Cecci Gori. Most of the talking was in Italian and none of it was about the film as far as I could tell. We left with the five-million-dollar budget. When we got back to New York and began prep the Italians wanted to know if they could just put the five million in my bank account. I said, "Are you fucking crazy?"

CRACK

You take the spoon and you mix a little coke with some baking soda, add a few drops of water, and heat it with a cigarette lighter. Whatever they added to it burns off and what's left is a small rock of pure cocaine. Preferably you have a glass pipe with a screen. You put it in there and you light it. It gives off the most beautiful smoke, the sweetest smell, and a taste that's even better. When pure cocaine is delivered directly to your lungs and brain it's like how you must feel in your mother's womb, safe, at peace with the whole world, a fullness in your stomach your body never forgets. Don't try it. Don't even think about it. Rip this recipe out of the book and burn it. You have to be Dante to describe where one hit leads you.

By the time we were making *Bad Lieutenant* I had a serious crack habit. It started off innocently enough, trying to get help for Chris Andrews, the editor of

Ms. 45 and a co-conspirator ever since. He was English with an upper-school British education, about ten years older than me and years ahead when it came to drinking. In fact I never did catch up with him. The hardest-drinking guys I ever met were all from England.

During *King of New York* my loft became a working office, with producers and lunch breaks and some degree of normalcy. Tony Redman was editing in the classic way, cutting on a flatbed during the day with all the assistants that go along with that job. I would work afternoons with Tony and come back around 10 p.m. to hook up with Chris, long after everyone had gone home. The serious work would start after Javi, our Colombian dealer and dearest friend, showed up with the righteous shit. For some reason Colombians are in awe of people with British accents. Chris was the only guy I knew who would weigh a gram right in front of them, pulling a miniature hand scale from his pocket. We would work Tony's cut against the music using new video equipment that Chris had introduced to us. Magic hour was 3:30 a.m., which gave us enough time to go down to The Cafeteria, a new bar around the corner on Union Square, for last call. A Long Island ice tea is a drink where they basically pour everything they got on the shelf into a glass. He would order three of them when we arrived and another three at one minute to four. I would order a bottle of red wine. That would get us through the second shift of editing, or at least till Mayin, Tony's Chinese assistant, would show up punctually at 7:30 a.m. to prepare for the next editing day. That was our cue to leave. She always asked me how the work went and I always said, "Incredible."

Chris called up one night saying he couldn't come to work, and then a second night, and by night three he wasn't even calling, so I went down to his ground-floor apartment on the corner of Avenue A and 11th. He answered the door and welcomed me into his apartment as if I came for tea. Julio was there, a young Puerto Rican coke dealer who we would let hang out in the editing room because he wanted to learn filmmaking. He was quiet, smart, attentive. But now I saw another Julio, an up-and-coming block manager with three young workers cooking crack in Chris's oven, filling little plastic bags with tiny ten-dollar pieces and throwing a chunk to Chris every so often. If it wasn't for the Uzi leaning against the wall you would think it was the back kitchen of a Dunkin' Donuts and they were making some of the fifty-two varieties. Needless to say Chris never came back to the editing room, and why should he. Getting high was the objective and getting laid was right up there with it. He was with his twenty-year-old Rican crack princess and all the rock they could smoke.

I smoked it at Chris's that night and the night after, and soon became a full-blown crackhead, chasing that blast for the next two years, dosed with fear, desire, paranoia, and alienation. I had moved with my wife Nancy and our two daughters to a beautiful brownstone on Perry Street. I would sit on the steps in front of my house sucking on a small glass pipe like I was having a cigarette. On the corner was the Perry Street AA meeting, and I would see the cats outside holding their giant containers of coffee and smoking cigarettes like their lives depended on it, cause they did. The cure was a hundred feet away but I couldn't see it and wouldn't see it for a long time.

As I descended further into my own hell, my career was taking off. It was the early '90s, and independent auteur NYC filmmaking was having its moment in the sun. Spike, Jarmusch, the Coen brothers, the Angelika Theater, Bob Shaye with New Line Cinema, and the Weinstein brothers with Miramax. But like my four-year-old once had me write on a cookie box, "Good things never last." Hollywood called and like fools we all listened. Buying a crack pipe at two in the morning on Sunset Blvd wasn't as easy as on the Lower East Side, but I found a way.

Over the next dozen or so years there were Chris sightings and crazy experiences with him, but no more editing. He died alone in a room in a funky no-star hotel off Eighth Avenue, a dude who cut for Godard and Nicholas Ray and passed on to me what film and music editing could be.

BODY SNATCHERS

I got a call from Mike Simpson, my agent at William Morris, to tell me, "You're not gonna believe it, but we got a job at Warner Bros."

"What?"

"They made the offer. Nicky can write it and you can bring your whole crew."

"What is it?" Stupidly I'm thinking maybe they had read one of our scripts that had been making the studio rounds and were interested in that.

"They are doing the second remake of *The Invasion of the Body Snatchers*. I'm in a meeting, I'll call you when I get out." Which in agent-speak means you got all the information you're getting. Mike was a cool, young dude from Texas of all places, probably the only Texan working at William Morris. He later went on to represent Tim Burton, Quentin Tarantino, and other hip directors, but I was literally his first client, so this was a big moment for the both of us. *The Invasion of the Body Snatchers Part 3* sounded like the stupidest fucking idea I ever heard for a film. Nancy stood there because she knew that agents didn't call to say hi. She wanted to hear what was up, then she wanted to hear how much. The how much turned out to be half a million dollars, and plenty for my crew, which was like winning two lotteries.

The limo arrives the next morning and that's the confirmation of the contract. Either you get in or you don't, but if you get in you are in. So at seven o'clock in the morning I kissed my little girls goodbye and was on my way to JFK. There you get greeted at the curb like Clint Eastwood and all the other directors of the Warner Bros. family. Nicky and I moved into the Chateau Marmont, they rented me a white Camaro, and life as a studio hack began.

A writer's room is the most idiotic invention known to man. It's the norm these days, but I think this was an early experiment. Lance Young, the executive in charge, sat at the head of the table, tall, lanky, mercilessly good-looking. At twenty-five he was one of the youngest studio executives in town, and so far he'd never had a film fail. He was a Harvard graduate, his sister was a soap opera star, and to top it off he was the role model of the new Altman film *The Player.* He drove the first SUV I'd ever seen. His clothes were expensive, casual, perfect. Everything about the guy said I shouldn't like him, but I did. Sitting next to him was Robert Solo, who produced *Part 2* and would end up writing a book about all this in which we were naturally the bad guys. Kimberly Brent, Solo's co-producer, was the expert on Hollywood cool, which actors were hot, what was in fashion, which movies were making money, a ticker tape of Hollywood culture that would change by the second. Then there was a guy who was called a story editor, as if Nicky needed one.

We would waste a whole day arguing over what words a teenage girl would or wouldn't say. This was a ludicrous way to make films. I walked out countless times, screaming at them and screaming at myself for being part of this bullshit. Asunta, Nicky's young wife right off the boat from Italy, would prepare us lunch at the Marmont. I would show up saying we were packing our bags and going back to NYC. Our fees probably added up to twice the GDP of the whole region between Rome and Naples where she's from. The look on her face made me finish her macaroni and go back for more torture. The creative side is a sacred place and this was blasphemy, but you can't quit on your own writer and crew. And the money was just too steep to walk out on.

For Christmas Lance bought me and Nicky each a copy of the classic *Hitchcock/Truffaut* book and underlined the passage explaining the difference between surprise and suspense. I tossed it into the Christmas fire in the big lobby of the Marmont. Nicky just laughed. He wouldn't let something like that bother him. I had read and memorized the book when I was sixteen, but reading it again at thirty I realized that Alfred jerked poor Truffaut off with every word out of his mouth, telling him the same bullshit stories he'd been telling his whole life. But he laid his truth on Truffaut about the New Wave and any other wave. "When they watch *Psycho* they scream just as loud in Tokyo as they do in New York." Speak with images, not words, because the meanings of words change in every translation. It's the pure cinema that speaks to everyone on the planet, the language of eight billion people.

Jack Finney's original serialized novel *The Body Snatchers* is a gem. He wrote it in the early '50s, between Nagasaki and the Cuban Missile Crisis, the heart of the Cold War. There's a brilliant scene where the lead character goes back to his childhood library, where the same librarian from when he was a boy asks if he needs help. But the woman, who gave him his first copy of *Huckleberry Finn* when he was eleven, is not the same. Then he gets it. She's been snatched.

For a scene like this to work, that element of familiarity has to be in place, so a doctor coming back to his small hometown is the perfect setup. Instead we had a family sent to an Army base where they knew no one, the father a scientist checking on the proper storage of toxic chemicals, some inane bullshit like that. There couldn't have been a more wrong setup for Finney's story, but that's what we had and we rolled with it. How Nicky managed to transcend all this and come up with the script he did is beyond me, where the aliens were not the usual bad guys but deliverers of a warning that the survival of the species depends on the abandonment of the ego.

I watched the two previous versions over and over, and though we stole the Donald Sutherland scream ending from Kaufman's and used that as a motif, it was Siegel's that taught me the most. Before the studio added that goofy opening and ending, accompanied by even goofier music, none of it his, Siegel's original began with an elegant shot of a train coming through the countryside, delivering the hero back to his hometown. Every shot after it was a doctoral in the use of the tripod as a source of movement when placed in the perfect spot and the action staged right. Classic Hollywood filmmaking.

We went with his long, choreographed takes, but were too into the moving camera coupled with orchestrated light changes. Bojan Bazelli, also the DP on *King of New York* and *China Girl*, studied at the Prague Film School. Back then they took the camera from you if you shot too many frames to slate a scene. But now he was going for it all, having them paint trees black to heighten the shadow effect. We shot in actual anamorphic, the lenses the size of living room furniture and enough lights to keep a small city going. It's all shit you can do when you have millions of dollars of studio money.

I called up Jack Finney because I had some questions I wanted answered and I wanted to hear him speak. Like Elmore he was as cool as they come, low-key, unassuming, brilliant. The lesson I took from him is he had zero resentment of the fact that three major films were made from his story, and all he got for it was 500 dollars. His attitude was he knew the deal going in, that he was selling his rights, and at the time he needed the money, and that's life in the film business. He was a little upset that he wasn't invited to be in the scene in Kaufman's movie that included actual San Francisco writers.

Warners feared he might have a legit profit position, no matter what a contract written in the early '50s said. I got a call from the lawyers soon after my call with Finney. As usual when it's serious the lawyers call direct. "Why are you talking to this guy?"

"I needed to get some script stuff figured out."

"Well figure it out yourself. What are you, out of your mind? Leave that guy alone."

Market research is key to the LA process. An independent contractor, whose name I forget, got paid a shitload of money to run what are called test screenings, which involved going into the San Fernando Valley, rounding up a theaterful of high school kids, showing them the movie, and then having them write out answers to a bunch of questions. From that they come up with a score, 100 being the ideal, which I'm sure even *Star Wars* didn't get. They randomly pick fifteen or twenty of these kids to keep after and further cross-examine, seeking some deeper truth. Then they go back into the editing room and recut the films around these notes. No bullshit, almost every film coming out of Hollywood is recut around notes given by sixteen-year-olds.

Our screening was at night so Bob Daly and Terry Semel, the real bosses of the studio, could be there. To put it in perspective, *The Fugitive,* starring Tommy Lee Jones, got a 91. Still Warner Bros. went back to work on it till it had a 95. Our film got a 46. I will give it to Daly for at least shaking my hand and saying good luck before I never saw him again. I drove home that night thinking about the last time I had a movie tested, and by the same guy. It was *Fear City.* We did it in Washington, DC, because that's where the investors came from. We got a 23 that night, which might have broken a record on the low end. So I figured we did twice as good with this one.

There was a meeting the next morning to discuss the results. Bruce Berman, the head of production, was there. Everyone involved just stared down at the table. I was the fall guy, which I should have been, because final cut or not I willed and bullied everyone into making the film I wanted, and we had just been handed a ridiculous grade and some nasty notes. I was leafing through them, amazed at the writing level of these high school kids. None of them could write a complete sentence, never mind the spelling. "Suh spense. Saspence. Suspentz." Obviously they didn't think there was enough suspense. Bruce was tactful and asked, "Don't you have any interest in these notes?" I said, "You should have spent the money for the screening teaching these kids English."

"You're not interested in the process, are you?" He was right. At that point I'd had enough of these people and their way of making films. And they'd had enough of me. They were also doing Oliver Stone's *JFK* and Spike Lee's *Malcolm X* and were having some hellacious battles with those two. I read an executive memo to Lance that said, "No more NYC auteur directors."

The good news was the studio had given up on the movie. They just wanted it done so they could toss it out on their international action track, so we finished it without further interference. I didn't hear anything from them for months, so I showed a cut to the guys I know at the Cannes Film Festival, normal practice, only this time they took it for the competition. We have premiered a lot of our films there, but this is still the only one of mine that has been in the main competition. I was still celebrating when I got a call from one of the lawyers. "You know we had big plans for the distribution of the film in the action market, but now that you've positioned it as an art film that's all out the window."

We didn't get any respect in Cannes either. The year before we had blown the place up with *Bad Lieutenant,* presented out of competition, and now I am getting all this heat about selling out working for the studios. One of the upsides to the Cannes, Berlin, or Venice festivals is you get to see your film perfectly projected on a huge light-balanced screen in a very dark theater with perfect Dolby surround. *Body Snatchers* in Scope, with a very expensive sound mix done by the young dudes who had just won an Academy Award for *Batman,* was a knockout.

We never attempted that style of filmmaking again. I credit Nicky, my editor Tony Redman, and my composer Joe Delia for dealing with these guys through the final stages of editing and saving this movie. We stand behind the film, but it was the last time I ever worked without final cut.

I was alone in an elevator with one of the executives at Universal during that time, and he clued me in on something. "You want to get a movie made here, make sure they can turn it into a ride afterward." So when you are out hustling scripts and carefully explaining your interesting storylines with even more interesting character arcs, think about this arc, a movie, then a ride.

BAD LIEUTENANT

ZOE

Walken was originally the Bad Lieutenant. We spent the week together in LA at the Marmont, working at fine-tuning the script. On the Sunday morning before I had to go back to New York and finish the prep, we had a meeting in my room, the producer Ed Pressman, Walken, and myself. Chris, in his usual direct way, said, "Ed, I know what Abel wants now, and I can't give it to him." Then he stood up, shook Ed's hand, and walked out. It took a moment for it to register with Ed. "Should I go after him?" I couldn't even muster an answer. Ed went racing off down the hall. I sat there thinking, damn, I already spent my director's fee.

Maybe I should have expected it. During that week Chris had said to me, "What's this fascination with religion? Come on, Christ? He's an overused literary device." Again Jay Julien came to the rescue. He gave the script to Harvey Keitel.

The teaching has to come from the teacher. It's handed down physically to the student. Like the begat part of the Bible when you get all those names, it's the same in the Buddhist texts. Proof of lineage. You can watch *Mean Streets* and *Raging Bull* all you want, but you're not going to get it just by watching. It's got to come direct from the source, hand-to-hand, face-to-face. The first thing Harvey said to me was, "There is a lot you guys can teach me, but there are things I can teach you." Who knows what he got from us, but I know what I got from this Brooklyn-born ex-marine with a fully opened heart. It was a hard-core approach to the discipline. I once bragged about how dedicated my crew was. He dismissed me, saying, "If someone isn't willing to pick his own ass and eat it they shouldn't be on the set."

He was in the midst of a brutal breakup with Lorraine Bracco, a woman he had been with longer than any other, the mother of his only daughter. So, unlike Walken, there was no comedy or irony to his approach. He knew how to put the spurs to the demons we were all riding and exorcise them in front of the camera. Penny Allen came with him. She was his acting coach, and wife of Charlie Laughton, who was Al Pacino's coach. A lot of directors are not cool with a coach around, but once I got what she was bringing I welcomed it with open arms. All that mattered was the next take. The exercises, hanging in the trailer between setups or after wrap, were all preparation for a focused on-camera performance.

Blondie is an icon from heaven because Debbie Harry is the real thing, brains and talent to go with the beauty, a street sense earned from a tough upbringing in North Jersey. She had this wisdom in her voice that sounded even better than the records everyone is still playing. I was hanging out with her during this period. I had insisted on driving my own car, a beat-up Chevrolet from the '70s someone gave me for the shoot. When we wrapped I would head straight for her townhouse in Chelsea, around the corner from the projects on Eighth Ave, where she would sit on the stoop waiting for me, surrounded by adoring young street kids. I'd hand her the keys and she'd park the car and score some crack for me from the dealers down the street while I went upstairs to drink the vodka in her freezer and cool out from the shoot. We were play-acting a kind of romance.

Dope was her trip. She understood what was written on every subway car and ghetto wall, "Crack is wack," but she didn't stress me on it. She drank the vodka with me and stayed up all night till I had to make it back to set. I wouldn't recommend sleeping only an hour before shooting all day, but that's what it was. I had already given the speech to the young crew on the first day of shooting. One hour after call time the cameras rolled, no matter who was there or wasn't, me, the DP, the actors, whoever. Shoot cars passing or crucifixes, but don't be standing around waiting for anyone. I don't recommend that either.

That morning I left Debbie's for Jersey, where we were shooting the church scenes, and got lost promptly after coming out of the Holland Tunnel. This is why directors are driven to the set. By the time I got there Kenny was filming inserts, waiting for me, pissed off. I walked out of the sunlight into that big dark church with "Fuck" scrawled across the altar and I thought, we shouldn't be doing this. A one-sentence offhand description in the script becomes something heavier in reality. A bad omen. The Jesuits say, "Give us the boy for his first seven years and you can have him for the rest of his life." Thirty years later I was still looking over my shoulder for a nun with her pointer stick. I later heard that the monsignor who gave us permission to shoot there was sent to a parish somewhere in Alaska because of it. I don't know if that's true but if it is I am making amends to him now.

I had told the art department to make sure that they got Jesus and the crucifixion right, put all the money on that, I'll make everything else work. Paul Hipp was Jesus. When he came out in makeup and wardrobe looking like Brooke Shields on a bad-hair day, I freaked. I spent half the morning micromanaging that. When we were done and he was looking good I told him to stay out of sight before we got thrown out of there. Later that day I went down to the basement where we had lunch and craft service set up. There was Hipp in his loincloth, a cigarette in his mouth, telling the monsignor about his Catholic school upbringing, both of them cracking up over it.

Harvey as a rule does not want the other actor to be off camera for his close shots. It had to be me or Penny. Harvey's rationale was "I don't even know the guy." Naturally Paul was disappointed. We usually cleared the set for his stuff anyway, so there was just essential crew there. Those church scenes were done with one camera and one take.

People declare that it is a film about redemption, or say I am a filmmaker that specializes in it. But redemption is a journey, not a destination. The Bad Lieutenant is a drug-ravaged dude having a hallucination, who's trying to scam his way out of a situation he brought on himself, bringing down everyone around him in the process. But the actor overrules the narrative. It's all a setup for Harvey, the man, to express something each of us has deep inside but so few can bring to the front. His humanity, which is essentially good, God-given or not.

Zoe was on fire the last day of the shoot. She had written those scenes, so she knew how to play them, and when it went off-page she was even more possessed.

She waited for the last setup to take the dope shot where you can actually see the dooj in action. It was her birthday of all things, so it was extra fully loaded and that look in the camera, that's the only way you're going to get that. It was what she was all about, total adoration of heroin, the miracle drug, the elixir of life, the keys to the kingdom, the total fucking delusion as physical reality.

She was born in Westchester County but direct from Planet X. I met her when she was seventeen. She had just left her loving home with an adoring mother and father, skipping her last year of high school, to start at Columbia University, a musical scholarship to boot. She was living with a group of classmates near Morningside Heights, with a young, cute philosophy major boyfriend who was always by her side. She was a brilliant writer even then. You couldn't mention an author she didn't know and couldn't pontificate on.

She sat and read the pages of *Ms. 45* in a flash and got all of what Nicky was writing about. She needed no direction. All she needed was Ritz crackers and milk, which I took away from her after she started busting out of her wardrobe. Funny looking back, because in the end she weighed ninety pounds soaking wet, with a syringe hanging out of her arm. She called it her cunt, the spot she jabbed the needle into, and she would let it hang there as she walked around the loft during the late-night *Bad Lieutenant* writing sessions. "That's my cunt, yes that's my cunt." She would sit down at the electric typewriter, blast out two full pages at lightning speed, pull them out of the machine, glance at them and laugh this beautiful, high-pitched musical laugh from that one-of-a-kind mouth with the red, red lipstick she wore in those last few years. Then she would roll them up, casually toss them in the trash and go back for more.

The script was short because that's how I wanted it. I'm writing for my crew and they only want what's necessary, skip the bullshit. She could have written a thousand pages on any scene in that film. The one long one we kept in was the nun's confession. The truth is when they gave the script to Keitel he threw it in the garbage before he got to page five. Thank god for Victor Argo, a regular actor of Scorsese's and ours and one of Harvey's closest friends, who begged him to keep reading it. It was that long scene in the confessional, way longer than in the final cut, that convinced him. Harvey felt it, the poetry, the crystal logic. It was her writing that got him to agree to do the movie.

The two long scenes in her kitchen with Harvey were shot back-to-back on that last afternoon. When you got the players and you are in the groove it's easy. Except for that scene of her, we weren't filming any real drug use. Harvey insisted on that. But we were certainly using them, except for Kenny, who had entered the program less than a year before and miraculously stayed sober during all that was going on. In the end it was a documentary, a how-to on destroying your life with alcohol and cocaine. When it was over I was in a desperate place.

HEROIN

NANCY

It was Javi who cured me. I was sitting one night in my brownstone getting high with him and Nancy, the two kids and their baby-sitter asleep up on the third floor. He could see I was in bad shape. He was also under instructions from his people back in Bogotá that it was time to start moving the dope they were now growing along with the coke. He laid out one line of smack next to the lines of coke on the small dinner plate. He said, "Here, do this, just don't do it three days in a row." Better advice was never given, but it was given to the wrong guy because skipping days is not my MO. I don't know what was going through my head at that moment because I had never ever done heroin up till then. I was forty-four years old.

I met Nancy in 1979 at the height of the punk rock downtown scene. She was friends with the just-arrived

Madonna and Keith Haring and Cookie Mueller and Basquiat and a million others all hanging out at Club 57 on St. Mark's. Jean-Michel was more than just a friend of hers. Everyone was in shiny suits with skinny ties. I was still a hippie outsider in jeans and cowboy boots and long hair, but I got hip quick. I went to some secondhand store and got the same suit I wore to my first high school dance, skintight, thin lapels, shiny, but I stopped at the skinny tie. When I left Catholic school as an eight-year-old I swore I would never put a tie around my neck again, and I didn't, except for my mother, at my church wedding, or when I ended up in court in front of a judge.

Nancy was sharing an apartment with a couple of friends, with gangs of sketchy people coming and going. It was near the Bowery, on the corner of Elizabeth and Broome above an Italian bakery, a neighborhood of boarded-up buildings and empty overgrown lots. I met her through a mutual friend. She came on a go-see for *Ms. 45*, and like every other long-term relationship I've had we were having sex before we had a chance to talk about it. Her grandmother was Sicilian and Nancy had those dark eyes and black black hair that was in fashion, natural or not. She had that look of knowledge kept to herself, beautiful, super smart, but could play dumb when it was to her advantage. She was a checkout girl in the supermarket at fourteen and had been working ever since. She was starring in an Off-Off Broadway play in the Village that I saw more than once. Sometime during the performance she would casually pull off the '50s bra that was part of her costume and just stare at the audience. Afterward I would be outside with five other guys also transfixed by her, all of us dressed in skinny suits, straight stage-door Johnny kind of shit. She would come out and talk to each of us, real cool, no diva stuff, and then just take her pick as the rest of us watched her walk down the street with the lucky guy. Then my turn came. She had a day job with Dior modeling fur coats in a Garment Center showroom, so she had her own money, plus she had a credit card from her father which I would hold in my hand like some kind of sacred object. She would take me to Raoul's, a French bistro on Prince Street, and we would sit at the bar, sharing a steak frites and a bottle of wine, surrounded by cool people she knew and an attentive bartender she probably knew too well but who cared. For a street rat like me this was heaven.

We had both been to the San Francisco Art Institute, although she was a registered student, studying acting and fine arts. She could draw and paint beautifully. We knew a lot of the same people and I thought this has to be a sign of something. It might have taken a whole month before we got to talking about where we grew up and she said Peekskill. I said, "What?" It turns out her mother taught second grade at the grammar school where I went. She went there too but because she was younger our only interaction was when, as a sixth grade monitor, I helped the kindergarten kids off the school bus. I actually held her hand making sure she didn't trip down the steps. After hearing shit like that I had to marry her.

It was eleven o'clock one sunny morning, not long after I met her. I was walking up the steps of her building, waving hello to her landlord, old man La Rosa, who was sweating over the brick ovens making the bread for that side of Little Italy. He didn't even have a storefront, but he wrapped up a loaf in white paper and handed it to me. I made it up the three flights and Nancy's door was open, which wasn't unusual. People were crashed out all over her apartment. The Mutants, a punk band from San Francisco, were in town and two of them were in bed with her. There was dope paraphernalia everywhere, syringes, bent black spoons, used cotton. I got the picture and left. She maintained her chippy dope habit on and off during the marriage, while keeping up with my alcohol and coke intake. She never touched the crack, thank god, but on more than one occasion I found her pocketbook full of empty dime bags of dope.

Now it's my turn. I'm looking at the dinner plate with the coke on one side and the heroin on the other, the fast and the slow as the Colombians would say. The first time you take it you throw up violently as your body reacts to the demon poison you are forcing upon it. Little by little the high rolls in. Read Byron or Burroughs if you want the poetic version.

I was quick to try everything else but heroin was my line in the sand, my Rubicon, till I crossed it, and then there was no going back. If you never tried it, don't. Don't even consider it. If there is nothing else you take from this book, take that. It got me like my first hit of reefer at sixteen or the first time having real sex, or that first crack blast two years earlier. This was life-changing, a physical and spiritual reboot of everything you hold sacred. It began a romantic period of new love, what Charlie Parker called his white lady. No more of what my Buddhist teachers politely call "sexual misconduct." I was back to sipping the good red wine, no longer slamming the Stolichnaya I stashed in the freezer. The nights and hundreds of dollars spent chasing a crack hit that never comes were over. Javi's remedy worked. I never smoked crack again. Now half of a ten-dollar bag of dope and I was good. I started playing my guitar again and listening to music. Billie Holiday, my favorite, those sweet early live records coming through the speakers, listening in the state she was singing in. I was human again, the conversations good and in depth, other people actually interesting to me. I was about to shoot a cool new film in our New York guerrilla style, right in the neighborhood. It was a film the prescient and observant Nicky St. John was calling *The Addiction.*

It was fall now, the best season in NYC, and I would

walk my two daughters to school at 7:30 in the morning and actually converse with their friends' famous and wealthy parents on the steps of the Little Red School House. I had all this going on for a mere ten dollars, taking one day off in every three. But a day is a long time for an addict. They say you chase the coke but the heroin chases you, and now the race was on, whose rightful conclusion is either jail, death, or total abstinence.

THE ADDICTION

MARLA

I began a love affair with Marla Hanson. She was graduating NYU and wanted in to the film business. *The Addiction* was centered around the Washington Square Park campus and she had all the right contacts there, so I made her the producer. She said to my wife, "I'm not trying to steal your husband," but I was long gone for this woman the minute I laid eyes on her. She wasn't tall, it ended up she wasn't even a model, but like the firemen at the station underneath my loft would say, "Of all the women that have come by here over the years, Marla was the one." She had that thing. She just slayed guys. They would lose their minds for her.

If you want to make guerrilla films you need guerrillas, and Marla stepped up. She kicked ass on that gig, getting us into places at NYU where people had never shot before. We were falling in love, or at least I was, working together blissfully through the shooting and editing. But my new addiction gave the relationship no hope. She would be asleep in bed and I would be in another room trying to get high without making noise, impossible with a woman who could hear people talking a block away. I was capable of obsession but incapable of loving. I put her on a pedestal and left her there. In the end she was looking for a real husband and I couldn't be that, even to my own wife.

Early in our relationship she thought she might be pregnant. I was happy with it. When I picked her up from the doctor's office and she said, "It's going to be twins," I almost drove into a light pole. It was Christmas week and she was on her way to visit her mother in Kansas City, where she was born, and said she would call with the phone number. By Christmas morning I was insane from not hearing from her. I called her best friend Joanie, who was no friend of mine, and asked if she had heard from Marla or knew her mother's number. She told me, "It's Christmas Eve, shouldn't you be focusing on your own family?" After a few more days of torture Marla called. She told me that she had just come back that night from burying the embryos of our children somewhere in the frozen ground out on the Kansas plain. She told me the miscarriage happened when she was straining to change a tire on her brother's car, and then she started bleeding, and that's basically all the story I heard as I sat speechless, watching my two little girls play around the Christmas tree.

Michael Halsband, a photographer and former boyfriend of hers, said she also told him she was pregnant when they were together. "That's just her way of testing you." Years later another dude told me that he had gone on a cruise with Marla and a group of friends the week that she was supposed to be in Kansas City with her mother. He thought I might still be angry with him, but by then the obsession had been lifted.

CARLITO'S WAY

Al Pacino saw *King of New York* and wanted to meet Larry Fishburne and me. We came to see Al after he had dinner at a club on Fifth Avenue near 23rd Street. Marty Bregman, Al's longtime manager slash producer, who was responsible for *Scarface* and many others, arranged it. Al was gracious and cool and it was a big moment for me and Fish. He told us he liked the film so much that after it ended he and his friends ran it again.

Soon after I got a call that they wanted me to direct their new film *Carlito's Way*. Got a call means that Marty Bregman asked my agent Mike Simpson if I would or would not be a problem. I'm sure Mike told Bregman whatever he wanted to hear. Then Marty called Jay Julien, my lawyer, and the real negotiations began. Jay was even older-school than Bregman. He drove a landing boat during the Normandy invasion and cut his teeth on Broadway representing three heroes of mine, Shelley Winters, Mike Gazzo, and Ben Gazzara. He repped De Niro and Scorsese in their early careers and now had Pesci, Walken, and Keitel. His office was right on Broadway and 43rd, high above Times Square, so he could look down on the other hustlers working the block.

Simpson and I would have taken that gig for scale, and been terrified to lose that, but if you survive the Invasion of Normandy you're not worried about blowing a deal. He told me we were doing Bregman and the studio a favor. Who knows what he told them or what he promised from his other clients, but at the end of the day he got me a million-dollar offer. I am now directing Al Pacino's new film and getting paid a million to do it. All is right in the world, yes? No, I needed to find a way to blow it.

The job began by meeting Al once a week at an apartment on 58th Street near Central Park. I got a taste of what the Actors Studio was about with Peter Weller, but I wasn't ready for it then. Now, after working with Harvey and Penny, I was. With Al, lines of dialogue are not just memorized, they are discussed, and the ideas behind them are discussed, and the events in our lives that relate to what is written are discussed. The script, or what they called "the text," is sacred. The actual dialogue is never spoken until the camera is rolling.

When Al could see I was getting restless, he would

give me a treat. He would act out a scene, never a Carlito scene, but one of the smaller characters, in this case a guy who had been shot up and was paralyzed. The rolling office chair became his old metal wheelchair. “He keeps his gun stashed under his blanket,” Al explained, “the diapers, the toilet paper under his seat . . .” And then he would transport you to a street corner in Spanish Harlem. It’s the hit I’m constantly chasing. I love the beautiful shots, I sit in awe of Welles and Kubrick, but it’s the acting that keeps me coming back.

Edwin Torres was a New York state supreme court judge who grew up in Spanish Harlem. He was a real NYC star, as comfortable in the Barrio as in Elaine’s or his lower Manhattan courthouse. He was not the guy you wanted to be standing in front of if you had been convicted of some nasty shit. He told one hard-core dude before sentencing, “Your parole officer hasn’t been born yet.”

He loved movies but he second-guessed everything he saw on the screen, dissecting out loud the continuity, motivation, location choice, till his wife one day turned to him and said, “If you don’t stop, I’m never going to another movie with you. If you’re such an expert, why don’t you write your own?” So he did. Working nights after court, he wrote a bitching short novel called *After Hours* that he imagined for the movies all the way, with a killer character named Carlito. Sometime in the late '70s Al read it and immediately bought the rights. Then he and Ed began the long, torturous journey of near misses, lawsuits, and heartache, until Bregman stepped in and did what he does best, steamroll whoever is standing between him and a start date. The ultimate manager/hustler ended their fifteen years of misery by getting a deal from Universal to finance and distribute it.

Pacino plays a conflicted gangster who just got out of a thirty-year jail sentence on a technicality, pulled off by his Jewish lawyer, to whom he now owes $75,000. His moral compass says he has to honor that debt. But how? As tough as he is, he can't handle the isolation of prison, and vows he will never go back. Out on the street his friends start talking to him. "It's 1975 now, it's cocaine not heroin, there are no Italians to deal with, just our own kind. Everything's done in Spanish, and with cocaine no one gets addicted so the police don't care."

Bregman thought he was a creative genius, which he wasn't, so we had some pretty heated discussions whenever he wanted to change things from the original story. Edwin and Al strangely kept silent through these. Edwin had his job as a sitting judge, so he wasn't always there and neither was Al. But everyone was present when Bregman came back from his meetings with the studio heads in LA. They wanted to know, "Why is 1975 so important? It would be cheaper to do it in the present." Why? Maybe because 1975 was the year *Newsweek* put cocaine on its front cover, announcing it was the new wonder work/party drug, non-addictive, the answer to everyone's problems. That was Carlito's rationale for going back to dealing. Now we're in the middle of a crack epidemic. They also wanted Carlito's love interest to be a go-go dancer instead of a teacher. One of my favorite elements of the story was Carlito's dream of a new life with the white substitute teacher he had a love affair with a few years before going to prison. He had visions of marrying her, taking her back to San Juan where he was born, and opening a Hertz Rental Car agency. That don't work with a go-go dancer.

Then Bregman delivered the knockout punch. "Did you ever hear of David Koepp?" Koepp was a hot young LA screenwriter who would go on to write *Jurassic Park* and a million other things. I was expecting Marty to come back with a start date, but instead he's coming back with a new screenwriter for a page-one rewrite of a script that was already righteous and ready to shoot.

I'd had enough of the whole fucking deal. I was about to go off on all of them. Instead I just split, out of his corner office and down a dark hallway. It was late and everybody else working there had gone home. Al came out to find me and you got to respect him for that. I got straight with him. "I'm tired of being the only one fighting for this." He said, "Abel, sometimes you got to . . ." Then he shifted his shoulders in a subtle Dion from the Belmonts dance move, looking right at me, just enough of a smile. I'm from where he's from, so I got the message without him having to say it out loud. Dude, you better learn to dance between the raindrops. We are two guys from nowhere. One of us is getting a million, and the other way more. What he did say was, "Let's give the kid a chance, see what he can do." Like with Walken or Keitel, I have too much respect to ever argue with him. All I said was, "We're ready to shoot, and now we're waiting on a page-one rewrite by a new writer. We might not get that for a year." Back when the film was on a fast track, a lawyer from the studio would call me before every rehearsal and say, "When you meet with Al, make sure he knows we are working toward a September start, ok?"

"Yeah, ok." Only with Al this September and next September are the same thing.

Bad Lieutenant went to Cannes, not in the main competition but in Directors' Fortnight, a sidebar event. It was the first public screening. Pressman literally had to bring the print over on the plane to get it there on time. As the film was about to start he tells me, "The guy at the lab said there are microphone reflections in the windshield of some of the shots." Well what was I supposed to do, jump onstage and apologize to the audience for it? Mic reflections or not, that film blew the mind of anyone who got in to see it.

The Hotel du Cap is not in Cannes, it's a thirty-minute ride up the coast and it's where the real players stay, their yachts parked out back. It used to be you could only pay in cash and plenty of it. I was with Gianni Nunnari and the rest of the guys who worked for Berlusconi, the group who would go on to do *Dangerous Game* with Madonna. Nancy, Ed, and I were about to leave when I decided to order a bottle of white wine for the ride home. Nancy said, "Don't do it." That was her psychic instinct. My response was, "We have to go all the way back to our hotel in that fucked-up car." All the way back meant a thirty-minute ride in the Mercedes Ed had been nice enough to rent for us for a week, with a driver. The A/C was broken, which I diva'd into some incredible tragedy. To sit in the back of that car with the Mediterranean Sea breeze blowing through an open window seemed impossible without a bottle of cold white wine in my hands.

The wine was on Nunnari's tab, and as the waiter was taking out the cork Ed came over to tell me that Tom Pollock, the head of Universal Pictures, wanted to speak to me. I said goodbye to my Italians and walked over to his table, the bottle still in my hand. Tom introduced us all around. He asked if we could talk in private. I left the bottle sitting on his table and we went outside into the garden. He wanted to talk about the new draft of *Carlito's Way*, which Koepp had just delivered and which Pollock thought was wonderful. I had read it on the flight and thought it was a travesty. I kept my opinion to myself and just nodded like a fucking idiot as he went on about how everyone was so excited about the script and the combination of Al and Marty and me. We went back to the table where I picked up my bottle, reflexively tucking it inside my white jacket, and headed for the car. That move of always taking your drink with you, whether it's a half-filled glass of double vodka or an unfinished Bud Light, is because in NYC you can't have alcohol open on the street. It's no big, everyone knows it, a reason we were always wearing sports jackets. I rode back to the Croisette, thinking about a check with seven digits and sucking on that wine like a baby on his mother's tit.

I was back in my house in NYC when I got a call from Simpson. It was a bit early for LA. He had a worried thing in his voice. "Was there a problem with a bottle of wine?" When you get fired from a million-dollar gig, a lot of people around you get hurt, starting with your wife and kids. I said to Mike, "I don't know what you're talking about." Nancy knew. She was holding Lucy on her lap, and the minute she heard wine she knew. An hour later Jay Julien called and it was game over.

"What's this about a bottle of wine you stole from Tom Pollock's table?" Unlike Mike he didn't wait for the answer. He just told me I had been fired and hung up. Those guys were getting 10 percent each from that money, so you can imagine how they felt. I sat there dazed as Nancy went on and on. "Why did you order that wine? What's wrong with you?"

What is wrong with me? A self-destructive nature? An innate feeling of unworthiness? A mistrust of success? What's wrong with me is that I'm an alcoholic. If I had any sense, which I didn't, I would have gone right down to the AA meeting on the corner. I would have gone in, kept my mouth shut, and listened. I would have called Kenny, who was a few years in recovery now. He was married with kids too. He started in AA to keep them, because his wife Dale was out the door with the whole gang unless he did something. He was the first one of us to get sober. I was the last. At the time his decision hardly sank in for me, just a distant feeling of, "Yeah, good, because he really needs it."

By now I had been using steady for twenty-five years. Hadn't I had enough? Why was the idea of stopping so completely foreign to me? I didn't make that call to Kenny or go to the corner meeting. I had another twenty years of what Paul Hipp calls "research" left in me.

A Hollywood project always needs a director assigned while it's in development, and in the end that's all I was. *Carlito's Way* was a film I was never going to direct.

Scarface had generated tons of money and *Miami Vice*, which was basically a spin-off, made Universal even more. With a potential payoff that high, no LA executive is going to take any chances in front of his Wall Street bosses with a different anything. You rehire the guys who did *Scarface*, the same actor, same producer, same director, and if the film doesn't live up to expectations, well that's life in the film business and maybe you keep your job. And *Carlito's Way* was no *Scarface*. Not by a mile.

Brian De Palma has always been an inspiring inside- and outside-the-box voice for me. Sean Penn I have a lot of respect for, but he didn't stand a chance. Carlito and the lawyer needed to be contemporaries. That's how it was written. That's how it needed to stay.

The films you don't make only exist in dreams. A dream of my crew and the budget we would have had, Torres next to me with Al, Keitel playing the Sean Penn role, the law and the street, the mid-'70s, the strange and mystifying bond in Edwin's story of reversal and reflection, and Carlito's need to achieve the middle way. We would have made something good. I don't care how much white wine we would have drunk.

WALKEN

JOHN HOLMES

THE THEATER

I told Walken a story about John Holmes, the '70s porno star with a 15-inch dick that was always hard. Holmes was from the Midwest and married a nurse when he got out of the Navy. They came out to California for some reason and ended up in Sherman Oaks. He was having lunch at a Denny's on Ventura Blvd and went in the bathroom to pee, and the guy peeing next to him was a producer making porno films in the Valley. He leaned over and said, "We can use a guy like you." Chris loved it. He said it was like Lana Turner at Schwab's drugstore.

Chris had a romantic Hollywood type thing in him, which he could never fulfill working with us. He should have been one of Hitchcock's leading men in movies like *To Catch a Thief* or *North by Northwest.* Most actors go through a script and count their lines. He would scratch his out. He also wrote scripts. He told me, "I got a script sent to me once and it was so bad I just turned it over and started writing my own on the back, checking to see how it's done every once in a while, till I filled all the pages." Something in the John Holmes story made him want to commission a script, maybe because he looked like him, who knows. I introduced him to Zoe. I wasn't making documentaries back then, but if I shot their first meeting I would have had the best one ever.

Zoe and her husband Robert Lund, a very nice guy and her longtime partner in addiction, had a sprawling rent-controlled apartment on the third floor of a brownstone just east of Fifth Avenue on 10th Street. He was a computer tech, the first one we ever met, and was making decent bread at it, all of it going to their habit. Their house was filled with big computers and printers, and naturally she was a whiz at them before most people knew what they were. Zoe kept rats, pet rats. I guess domesticated white mice is the term you use. She had about fifty of them, mothers, babies, some in cages, some she let run free. That's where I took Walken for the meeting. I have seen plenty of rats living in NYC and I have this thing about them running up the inside of your pant leg to bite your dick. It's an Orwellian kind of thing. So whenever I went to Zoe's I gaff-taped the bottom of my pants to my boots, but this time with Chris I didn't. I just took my chances. I don't think he really believed me until we got there, and they were everywhere. Walken was dressed in his usual blacks and so was she, in her own version of Gypsy freak, her bright red lipstick even brighter against her pure white skin which actually matched Walken's. She chain-smoked these long, brown filter-tip menthol cigarettes called Mores. I made sure I came with three or four packs on me so I wouldn't have to go running out looking for them mid-meeting. She would intersperse the script talk with feeding the baby mice out of an eyedropper filled with milk, giving kisses to her favorites, some sitting on top of a pile of books looking straight at you. Give Chris credit, he never batted an eye, but we also never had a script meeting there again. He laid out the idea, as usual using as few words as possible. Zoe, in pure junkie form, only wanted to know how much she was getting and if she could get a few hundred of it right now, which I had begged her not to do.

I don't have any copies left of her original draft, but like the other scripts she wrote solely on her own it came in at around 250 pages on legal-sized paper, small type, wall-to-wall margins, a sea of black from beginning to end. The printer complained about how much ink he needed to make copies. Her scripts went beyond the narrative. She laid out the intent and emotion of the smallest characters, detailing the wardrobes of extras, describing every prop. They were brilliant, she was brilliant, but in my business they were useless. Jay Julien was the only one who could get through them. He loved her crazy off-the-wall sex scenes. He even acted one out for me where an old guy, enamored with the girl sitting ready in his bed, undressed in front of her and did a running swan dive on top of her. That one never left his mind.

Chris read her Holmes script and hated all of it. He was not interested in sleazy Hollywood or the Wonderland murders or the specifics of the porno business. We did not get into any revision bullshit. He paid her, then sat down and wrote it himself.

I have never had so much buzz surrounding a film I didn't make as the John Holmes story. Chris called me up and asked if I would meet him for lunch the next day at Columbus, a bar restaurant owned and run by the late Paulie Herman, all the way on the Upper West Side. It was the hangout of the more successful NYC actors and their hangers-on. It was almost a private club. I got there at one in the afternoon and Chris was sitting with Eric Roberts and Nicky D. Eric was a friend and neighbor of Chris's in Connecticut. Nicky is an actor who is somewhere in all my movies, a 6' 7" Jersey dude who played basketball for Lou Carnesecca at St. John's University. See *Light Sleeper* by Paul Schrader, where Dafoe plays a drug dealer, a reasonable facsimile of him. He was a dear friend of mine and Chris's, and he came with the blow.

On the other side of the room was Wesley Snipes with a bunch of stunt guys celebrating the wrap of their movie. I went over to say hi and saw that the table was sagging from all the food they had ordered. The only thing on our table was a bottle of wine and some unopened menus, not even bread, each of us taking turns going to the bathroom. The waiter comes back to take our order. Chris puts the menu down and just orders another bottle of wine. In usual Walken fashion he gets right to the point. "I want you to meet Eric. He's going to be the star of the film." It was the first time he had shared with me that he had no intention of playing John Holmes. In his mind it was always Eric's part. I realized he was never interested in John Holmes as more than some crazy metaphor for fame and making it in show business.

In the end the project morphed into a one-man show about fucking Elvis Presley, which Chris performed on a couple of magical Christmas weekends down at Joseph Papp's theater. An inimitable performance. Who knows if there is any record of that.

It was the same Off Broadway theater where I saw Robert De Niro whipping the statue of a Madonna with his rosary beads in a play with Michael Carmine and Paul Calderón. At the Circle in the Square I watched Pacino bursting out of nowhere, screaming "Judy Judy Judy" in Mamet's *American Buffalo.* Keitel with Bill Hurt in another Mamet piece. Dafoe in the garage on Wooster Street in *Hairy Ape.* The movies smoke, but with the theater, you're in the room with them. It is what we are trying for in our use of long takes and the hard law of no re-shoots, looking for something Harvey would call the "emmis," the talisman, the alchemy, to find Alexander Pope's "grace beyond the reach of art." Ben Gazzara as a stand-in for another actor one night in New Haven, again with Al, in a play called *Chinese Coffee.* Ben barely knew the lines, but he knew how to spin that magic. The two of them all alone for ninety minutes, which felt like thirty seconds. I have tried it. I have directed five legitimate theater pieces, and one was a bigger disaster than the next. I am ready to try again.

When my mother realized there was no turning back for me in show business, she said, "There's a broken heart for every light on Broadway." What she didn't tell me was that Broadway starts on 233rd Street in the Bronx and doesn't stop till the courthouse in downtown Manhattan.

Zoe died in Paris from the heart infection long-time needle junkies get. She left Robert for some French dude, and when she told him she was leaving he grabbed her favorite rat, brought it downstairs, and stomped it to death in the middle of 10th Street while she watched from the window. She had finally started doing the coke that she was smuggling to France to pay for her dope habit, breaking her long-time rule that coke is for losers. She was thirty-nine.

Jimmy Hayden was the young actor in *American*

Buffalo and the club owner with the blue eyes in Sergio Leone's *Once Upon a Time in America.* He was going to star in my movie *Fear City,* and hopefully many others. He had it all going on, including a serious heroin addiction. He would stand up mid-sentence and take off on his motorcycle, or nod out mid-conversation as we were planning our assault on Hollywood. He overdosed in NYC soon after. Jamie Remar, who replaced him as my muse, was also strung out and ready to ride his motorcycle into oblivion. He miraculously found recovery and was a big help in mine. Michael Carmine, one of the sweetest, most gifted actors ever, was not so lucky. Neither was Chris Penn.

One time Walken and I were leaving my house in the Village for his apartment near the Museum of Natural History. He was performing Shakespeare in the Park later that night. I thought he had just come from his country house up in Connecticut, so I was following him to his car. After we walked around the same block twice I said, "Chris, did you forget where you parked?" He said, "I don't have a car. I was following you." Iago has more spoken lines than almost any Shakespeare character. I am thinking how is he going to pull this off, especially after we smoked a couple of j's of the super weed he always carried around. I could barely find Central Park, never mind where I was supposed to sit, but he came onstage rocking. In the middle of the play gunshots rang out in the distance. This was the early '90s. Everyone onstage and in the audience pretended it wasn't happening, except for him. He stopped, turned his back to listen, and when all the gunshots were over he went back to the play. Another time, and this was a Broadway premiere, a woman in the front row dropped her playbill on the edge of the stage and it tumbled forward into a circle of light. Everyone again acted as if it hadn't happened, that they didn't hear the woman groan, or that the big yellow page was just part of Ibsen's drawing room. When Chris got to that side of the stage he leaned down, picked it up, and kindly handed it back to her.

Chris and I were rehearsing at the Chateau Marmont when Pacino called and asked if he could find an hour with him to work on something he was doing. "I hate to disturb you," he said. Al was always humble like that. They went in the bedroom together and I could hear them talking in modern street talk, loud nasty shit about killing people and other crazy stuff. It was a Shakespeare play. That was their way of preparing, fascinating even from the other side of the door.

A few years later Joseph Papp was going to do every Shakespeare play in one three-year push. *Timon of Athens* was the one no one wanted to do. I ran into Papp at a party and asked him if he would be interested in Chris playing Timon with me directing. I had this idea about doing it in the vernacular I heard Chris and Al using. He said, "For sure," relieved to finally get that play set up. I told Chris the news, but he was dismissive. "Sure, give Timon to Walken." Then I explained my idea that it would start in Trump Tower and end up in a crackhouse in Harlem, and he would vamp on the dialogue like he did with Al that day at the Marmont. "Are you crazy? People come to hear the language, the words. You can't do that, not at a Shakespeare festival. You have to give them his words."

"But I don't relate to his words."

"You will when I say them."

KUBRICK

They had a new 70mm version of *2001* and for some reason it was the one Kubrick film I had missed. I went in the afternoon to the Ziegfeld Theatre on 55th Street off of Sixth Avenue, which had as good a projection and sound as you were going to get. Naturally I got my mind blown. I am sure I was high for some of it, but the film got you high. Like all Kubrick it was immersive and perfect and cool and inspiring, humbling more than anything. Ten years later I was visiting a girlfriend up in Vermont. She had a cabin in the middle of nowhere and one night a real winter storm blew in. Stuck in that cabin with her asleep and me wide awake, *2001* came on TV. She had a 12-inch black-and-white set with one tiny speaker next to the volume knob. I lay on the bunk bed a foot from that screen and watched the movie all over again. It had the same effect. His graphic formality emanated from the center of the frame, regardless of whatever pan and scan they did. The mono mix coming through the tiny tin speaker was all you needed. It's the ideas in that mix that make it.

I saw *Full Metal Jacket* at the Ziegfeld too, this time at the premiere with Matt Modine, who I didn't know at the time, sitting in the row in front of me with the other young actors from the movie. When Scorsese showed up it was showtime. I was thinking, what is Kubrick going to do to blow us away now using the new Dolby technology, all that enriched low end, which he basically invented for *2001*. The whole first hour was a single human voice screaming at you dead center. When the music finally kicks in, the bass of that Nancy Sinatra song, it sounds like the first time music was ever used in a movie.

I saw *The Shining* with my mother at the cinema in the shopping center in Peekskill. My father had just died and this was a way to chill out from three grueling days of the Italian-style wake and funeral. My mother loved movies. She grew up in the great Loews and RKOs of the Bronx, Stanley's home turf. She took me to *Bambi*, my first one, and later when I was older she would bring me and my sister with her to the afternoon movies that were made for housewives of the '50s. There I saw Douglas Sirk's outrageous *Imitation of Life* in a theater full of sobbing women. My mother was the kind of person who had a movie figured out by the time it was half over. I, on the other hand, am always surprised by whatever idiot thing comes next. So in the Kubrick film she knew Jack was going to eventually try to off the family. With the ghost of my father in that theater, my mother and I rooted for Shelley Duvall to triumph over that alcoholic energy. I adore Shelley Duvall.

THE FUNERAL

CHRIS PENN

I wrote a song called "Tonight Will Be the Night" for the soundtrack of *The Funeral.* It was a rip-off of Dylan's "Blind Willie McTell." We couldn't afford "Blind Willie McTell" because we spent the whole music budget buying Billie Holiday's "Gloomy Sunday." So it was up to my composer Joe Delia and Nicky St. John and me to come up with the rest of the songs for the movie. I was no longer living with Nancy and the kids, and I wrote the song thinking especially of my four-year-old. I will never make a living as a songwriter, but at least Joey liked it and Chris Penn loved it. He would belt it out when it was just me and him rehearsing at my house, me strumming along on guitar.

We were shooting in a bar in Harlem that still looked like it could be 1934. The scene was first up after lunch so during the break Joe, Chris, and the band did one last run-through. From a table on the side I watched the beauty of the whole process, the magic of the moment arriving, all the work and preparation coalescing. Everyone was in wardrobe, the lights set. The urgency that comes with knowing you are going to lay this down for the first and last time brings the clarity. I heard the lines I had been looking for, and was scratching out words and putting in the right ones when a giant hand slammed down on mine. It was Chris and he was right in my face. He said I was reminding him of his mother, how she painted beautiful things but would ruin them in her pursuit of perfection. It would make him crazy as a child, watching with frustration as she kept changing what he saw as perfect. I wasn't going to argue with him, and not because he was a big scary dude, but because he was the one who had to deliver the song.

Chris sang the shit out of it, and that performance is a reason I don't like watching my movies. Seeing him so young and alive in that moment, hugging his movie brothers Vinny and Walken, his eyes shining from some inner light, the rare gift of certain actors. It kills me. How could I have reached out to him, I was as lost as he was. Why him at forty, not me?

We almost killed Vinny Gallo on that film, but he bravely came back to do his last scene with what was officially a broken nose, but what I knew was a hairline fracture of his skull. It was a night shoot in a '30s-style house we did up somewhere in Brooklyn. It was with Isabella Rossellini, Chris Penn, and Amber Smith, a cool Marilyn look and act alike, and our usual shooting crew of volatile people. It was the kind of scene that read beautifully on the page but was not working at all on the set. When it's not happening it's not happening, and you don't have to be Orson Welles to know it but you have to be Orson Welles to fix it. We did a few takes and it kept getting worse. My go-to move in these situations is to call lunch, but they told me lunch wouldn't be ready for half an hour, so we go again. The scene begins and Penn, either blowing the cue or having a moment of divine brilliance, enters way early from the stairs above. The whole dynamic of the scene changes, everyone is thrown off, and Chris is now enraged from the get-go. Suddenly it's a working, rocking scene, and all of us watching are on edge, caught up in the drama of Nicky's mythically dysfunctional family. Penn grabs Gallo by the shirt and pulls him up off his feet, threatening to punch him out, hairline fracture or not, written or not, freewheeling, fuck the marks, fuck the lines, Kelsch rolling with the punches, getting it all. Somebody might have called cut, and now as an extra reward lunch was ready. They called it, but Isabella was having none of it. For the first time since we began shooting she spoke up. Her anger was quiet but strong. She said the script was beautiful, and us playing fast and loose was destroying it. And the language, fuck, fuck, fuck, that Chris was shouting, and me adding to it from behind the camera, was an insult to the whole process. She said she was coming to the set scared, which she had never felt before in her life. No one spoke. I stood looking at her, the daughter of Roberto Rossellini, one of the hands-down greatest directors, and thought, that's some heavy shit. Long, long silence, till someone said, "Can we please go to lunch?" We began to head outside for some air when Chris shouted, "Nobody move, anybody fucking move I'll kill them!" We all turned back around. Once again real life on a movie set trumps the written drama. Penn wanted to apologize to her, and he wanted to do it in front of all of us. Tears coming down his face, he asked her to forgive him and me. Then he turned to Nicky and told him he was sorry if he in any way disrespected the script. Very impressive moment.

Chris was the kind of guy you wouldn't hear from for a long time, then you'd get a call out of nowhere, no hello, no how ya been, right in the middle of a story. "You know what he did? You know what this motherfucker did? He fired me right in front of our mother!" It took a while to get the whole story, which might have gone like this. Sean was planning a movie with both Brando and Nicholson. They were doing table readings. As a great brother he invites

Chris, basically offering him a role in the movie. The first day Chris is twenty minutes late. Second day he keeps Sean, Marlon, and Jack waiting for forty minutes. Third day he's an hour late and arrives covered in blood. He was driving over Laurel Canyon and got into some dispute with another driver. At a stoplight Chris got out of his car, opened his trunk, took out a 4 iron from his golf bag and proceeded to smash the windshield of the other guy's car. He either got hit by flying glass or his own golf club, who knows. He asks me if it was fair for Sean to fire him over something like that. Good question. "Then what happened?" I asked. "I beat the snot out of him," was the answer.

Way later, long after Chris died, I was at a film festival in Sarajevo being interviewed by a local journalist. All he wanted to talk about was Chris. The journalist told me that when he was younger he had gone to LA hoping to have a career as a screenwriter. He started off working for a private cab company. One night he drove Chris home and they hit it off. From then on, when Chris called the car service, he would ask for "that fucking Russian guy." One night the dude worked up the courage to ask Chris if he would read one of his scripts. Chris said yeah, no problem, just toss it over the railing of the balcony of my second-floor apartment. A couple of months later Chris asked the car service to send "the Russian guy" to pick up his takeout order from a Mexican restaurant. The journalist said it was so much food he thought there was going to be a party, but when he got upstairs Chris was all alone. The journalist stood in his kitchen, then looked out onto the balcony. It was filled with scripts, unopened, unread, a massive pile of them left under the rain and sun.

BUSTED 2

I had left Nancy and the kids for Marla. She left me for nobody and was living alone in the Chelsea Hotel. Nancy was in love with our Colombian dealer Antonio, who was now living with her and the kids. We were all within a few blocks of each other, but I felt more alone than I've ever felt in my life. The guys were preparing the sound mix of *The Blackout* in the front room of the loft, which is where we were doing the editing. I was living in the back. As usual, by the time we got to that stage of the post-production I was out of money. I was also out of any desire or energy to jump-start the next project. I would hit these poor dialogue cutters up for enough to score.

I started walking toward Rivington Street, looking for a cab, when I see Antonio and his cousin Javi fly by in my car, which I guess went with my wife. Magic hour is as beautiful in downtown Manhattan as anywhere, but it is also the time of day the cab drivers changed shifts, so I had plenty of time to enjoy it while I searched for one. I walked deeper into the Lower East Side, getting more dopesick and pissed off the farther I got, when like magic a Checker cab pulled right up to the light. I jumped in. It was a Russian dude, playing Russian folk music on his cassette player, happy as hell on life and talking up a storm. My whole perspective on the world changed. I got money and I got a ride taking me to a guaranteed score, so I'm singing with him as we're speeding along.

The first rule of copping drugs is don't let the cab wait for you, especially in that neighborhood, because it draws the cops. The transaction with Leonard, my dealer, would happen right in his doorway and usually lasted five seconds. I didn't want to be looking for another cab, so I told the driver to wait just half a minute. Bad move. Leonard answered the door with a tragic look on his face. His younger sister, who I knew, was in the hospital, and he was on the phone talking to the doctor. So our five-second transaction became ten minutes. I waited. I got the five bags of dope I needed and turned back to the street. No cab. I am back to pissed-off mode, cursing this Russian motherfucker as I walk up the block back to civilization.

Rule 2 is keep the shit in your hand, so in case of trouble you can just toss it, though it would have to be big trouble before I tossed five bags of Leonard's dope. I get to the corner, and who's standing in front of the deli in a conversation with two guys but my Russian cabbie. I jump right in the back of the cab, screaming, "What the fuck man, I told you to wait!" One of the two, a young Chinese dude, turned too quick and was too tough-looking to be anything but what he was, an undercover cop. His partner, an older white guy in jeans and sneakers, was just as obvious if I was paying any attention. Now I'm stuck in the back of the cab, the bags still in my hand. The older one leans in the window and tells me to get out. I slide over to the other side of the cab, thinking I can dump the bags if I get out that way, except the Chinese dude is waiting for me. "He said get out that door," and that's what I did. The older one sees right away that I am holding something, and puts his hand around my wrist. "Open your hand." I look down and for a moment my fear turned to logic. What if I don't open my hand? What if he forces it open? Would that be unlawful search and seizure in front of a judge? He might have been thinking the same thing because we stood for a long second before I realized how ridiculous this was. I was busted. I opened my hand. He took the bags from me. "Where did you get this?"

"I don't know, some dude on the street."

"The driver said you went into a building. Which one, what apartment number?" Leonard was a little scarier than these cops, a serious dealer with plenty of shit in his place, and guns. He was also a good friend and a very nice guy who loved films. I was not about to give him up. Instead I went for my editing team, two young dudes whose vice was drinking a beer after work. I told them, "I was buying it for someone else, the guys who work for me." The Chinese guy threw me against the wall and started ripping at my pockets, to the utter delight of the teenage Puerto Ricans watching. They were getting a big kick out of an older white guy getting the treatment usually reserved for them. The cop found a straw in my pocket, so there went my story. "This is what, what you snort your coke through after you do that other shit?" Good guess. My only identification was my Directors Guild card, of all things, which slowed them down a bit as they tried to figure out what it was. Then the handcuffs came on, behind my back. That click is a game changer, trust me, so I went right for the mercy card. "Listen, I'm a film director. You ever hear of *King of New York*? *Bad Lieutenant*? I just started using this shit. I was told to come to this block and the kids will walk right up to you. I didn't go into no building." They were still listening, so I went for it all. "I got a wife and two little girls and if I get busted my career and their lives are over." At that moment a patrol car with two uniformed cops pulled up. The driver was female, hooting and hollering at seeing some action. The older one went over to their car, saying, "Wait till you hear who we've got." And now the Chinese cop gets right in my face. "*Bad Lieutenant,* that film sucks, you know that? You know what I'm saying, that film is a piece of shit." Well everyone's entitled to his opinion and maybe you'll like the next one better, would be my usual response. But I just nodded in agreement.

The squad car pulls off and the older guy comes back. He says to me, "What was the name of Wesley Snipes' partner in *King of New York*?" It was a test. I said, "David Caruso." He gave me my DGA card back and took the handcuffs off. They told me to get in the back of their unmarked car, and off we went. They had the radio playing music and they were talking shit, not about me, just laughing and joking like I wasn't even in the car. We had driven for a while like this when I realized we had passed the precinct. Where were we going? I started having visions of these two beating the shit out of me or worse, when the older one, who was driving, jerked the car up and over the corner of the curb. He spun around and grabbed my left hand, then shoved the five bags into my right hand. "Open the door and throw them down the sewer." And that's exactly what I did. I closed the door and we took off uptown to 14th Street, the border of their precinct. He didn't even turn around this time. "We ever see you in this neighborhood again, even just walking down the street, we're gonna throw you right the fuck in jail. You got it?" I got it. They made an illegal U-turn and burned off into their night while I crossed 14th and walked a couple more blocks to a pay phone to call Leonard and let him know what happened. He was cool. I was still dopesick but not as much, and definitely not worrying about feeling lonely.

NICKY

NEW ROSE HOTEL

ASIA

Nick St. John was a pseudonym for his very Southern Italian last name. We all took pseudonyms during the porno days, when there was real risk of interstate transport and other offenses, but his stuck. His family also came from outside Napoli, which bonded us further, but he was 100 percent Italian as opposed to my half-breed self. We were both fourteen when we met, and he was already writing and painting and playing the guitar. I was into music, at least what was on AM radio, but he was listening to Woody Guthrie and Hank Williams and the first Dylan albums. He was one of the first people I knew to even have albums, not just 45s. Our friendship was immediate and strong, as young teenage friendships can be. I never met anyone like him and haven't since. He was

Pasolini-like, short, skinny, and already had to shave every day. He dressed like no one else. In our high school we all dressed pretty much alike, but he was a freak. He played in a rock band, sang beautifully, and was already having crazy sexual experiences. I realized from him that you could create, you didn't have to wait, you could satisfy that urge with a pen or a paintbrush or a guitar or whatever. The camera came a little later, but the idea of leading a creative life began with him. We hung out in the cemetery across from his house and drank cheap wine and talked and played guitar and dreamt big dreams.

You have to know Peekskill to know Putnam Valley, which is where he came from. Peekskill was built on a big beautiful bend of the Hudson River. In the '60s my end of town was half rural and half suburbia, but when you got to the end of Hollowbrook Road and made a left over the Hollow Brook itself, you were basically in Appalachia. This is where Nicky grew up, living with some real crazy hillbillies. It was all farm animals and George Jones playing in hick bars. The kids went to their own grammar school, so when they hooked up with the rest of us at the communal high school it was pretty funny. You would hear "They're from the Valley," and everyone got it.

Our high school was progressive enough that by the time Nicky and I were seniors there was a new Humanities class where you would get a grade for just being creative. They showed *Citizen Kane* on the same 16mm projector I was forced to watch football practices on back in ninth and tenth grade, when I played on the Junior Varsity team. But I was long past playing football now. I was a long-haired, antiwar, pot-smoking little rebel on the day they pulled down the screen above the blackboard, opened up some cans of film, and ran the movie. It entranced me. The "How the fuck do they do that" feeling that I still get when I watch something virtuosic. Our cool history professor, an amateur photographer, tried to explain the pyrotechnics involved, but even he didn't get what Welles and his cinematographer Gregg Toland were up to.

Stanley Kubrick told Spielberg, "You can't just make a film, you need to reinvent the cinema." Make the technical shit meet your vision, not the other way around, and if it doesn't exist, build it. I had the 8mm camera my uncle Bobo had given me, and we were off to the races.

My first film was a short based on "The Myth of Sisyphus," of all things. Caldor was the name of the Walmart-like store in the local shopping center. It actually had a camera department, and that's where you bought film and then brought it to be developed. It was run by a crazy middle-aged movie director who we called "The Doctor," because that's what he called everybody, "Doctor." I learned more from him than from half my future film professors. When a can of film came back flashed because the kid we trusted to load it didn't know how, he told me, "You don't need jerkoffs like that around when you're trying to make movies." Still good advice.

William Gibson stuck "New Rose Hotel" in the middle of a collection of short stories called *Burning Chrome.* Eight pages containing multitudes. It defied my concept of story, shattered every handhold of artistic convention I had built for myself. Every word counted and the sum was infinite, writing like quantum physics, not what is but what is possible, every reread a different story. Sandii, the protagonist, is drawn so clear you can taste her. Why can't we make movies like this, where the viewer becomes the final piece of the equation?

Gibson's story was structured in a prism of flashbacks, the same event happening multiple times. Perfect for independent low-budget filmmaking and the way of our actors. Walken never did a take the same way twice. For him it's cheating, it's rehearsing on film. Every take would come from such a different place. We would usually stop at three. In the editing room of *King of New York* or *The Funeral* you had the option of many different movies. In *New Rose* we could use his different takes in the flashback sequences to give new meaning to the scene, the heart of the William Gibson experience. It all made clear simple sense to me but even Walken, a true genius, was not getting it, and definitely not poor Ed Pressman or any of our line producers. At the end of the shooting everyone was convinced we did not have enough scenes for a feature-length film. Fuck them all, I have final cut and enough blow, dope, and alcohol to pursue the ideal.

The Hollywood side of the story goes like this. Pressman bought the rights to Gibson's short story when, for a brief time, cyberpunk was a catchphrase that flew with the studios, Gibson its young inventor. His novel *Neuromancer* was making money at the box office. *Blade Runner* had been out for a while, its street cred growing each year, though sadly its author, the great Philip K. Dick, had died on the eve of its release. Pressman wanted Schwarzenegger to play the lead role of the crippled Fox, trying to turn *New Rose* into an action piece. The agents pushed Ed to hire Arnold's friend to write a script for 300k, and that would ensure Arnold at least reading it. Then they hired Kathryn Bigelow for another exorbitant fee to develop and direct. To make a long, sad story short, after two years Kathryn had sense enough to move on, Arnold passed, and Ed was left holding a very expensive bag. That's when he called us.

I read one of the three scripts that had been generated, which was more than enough. They had turned this eight-page gem into another bullshit Hollywood action read, where every foot chase and fight is laid out shot by ridiculous shot. A third of the way through a script like that you feel like you're getting your own ass kicked. In Gibson's story, Fox was crippled from a revenge hit-and-run and was barely walking with a cane, never mind jumping off buildings and beating the shit out of people on the way down.

The breakfast meeting at the Carlyle Hotel was at 8 a.m., with Pressman close to tears over the money he had lost. He implored Nicky and me to help him save the situation with the $40,000 he had left for another screenplay. The natural response was, "Why didn't you come to us in the first place, when you still had all that money?" But it was too early in the morning for me to put that sentence together. It wasn't too early for Nicky, who has been getting up early his whole life. He got the picture and understood the hustle. He is not a guy you insult, and that's what this was, no matter how you look at it.

Without anyone, including me, realizing it, Nicky left the table and took the train back to Peekskill. It wasn't just about Pressman, it was about me and how I let a once-innocent dream of making films together turn inside out. Nicky never touched drugs. He was devout in his belief in God. He had watched me spin off into the darkness, and maybe me leaving my wife and children was the final stroke. He did not like where the business was taking him either, and so, at our moneymaking zenith, he turned his back on the whole thing, back to his simple country life, his wife and family, and his true calling, teaching handicapped children. I never saw him again.

I had one position with Pressman, if we do the short story as written I'm in, otherwise forget it. I got Walken and Dafoe involved and so Pressman agreed. Willem and I knew each other from downtown and had discussed doing things together for a while. This would be the first.

A "key element" in a movie contract is a component without which the finance and insurance will not go forward, which in this case was me, Dafoe, and Walken. But Willem and I knew better. We needed the girl, a twenty-year-old as written, who could go toe-to-toe with them and be up for the sex.

Dario Argento was a kind of mythic presence for us, from the time we saw *Suspiria* at our local drive-in. The fact that his own band Goblin scored it made it even better. So when his daughter Asia's name came up, highly recommended by who knows, we were interested. The production office spoke to her agent and set up the call.

"Ciao, my name is Abel and I am a director, and . . ." She broke in right there, taking over the call and everything else between us ever since. She knew all about me since she was five years old, and yes, she wanted to do the movie. I said because of the delicacy surrounding the rating and her age and whatever other bullshit they told me to say, the casting people would get in touch and bring her and a chaperone to NYC. That's the word that was being used, chaperone. The others who we thought could pull this off were Chloë Sevigny, Milla Jovovich, and a French actress named Virginie Ledoyen. Virginie came from Paris with her aunt and was game, but in the end her boyfriend freaked at the thought of her working with me and Willem and my crew, so she went back to Paris.

A few days later on a Friday night about ten o'clock I get a call from Asia. I told her again she needed her agent to call the casting office and they would set up a date to bring her to New York. She said, "I'm down the block from you with a bottle of vodka. What's your buzzer number?" I called Willem and said, "You need to get over here." I was officially separated from Nancy and living a few blocks west of her and the kids in Chelsea. There were people around my place that night and someone had a video camera and captured some of what went on. It was harmless, but far from any standard audition. By the time she left, Willem and I agreed we had our Sandii.

About a month later, a Friday, Asia arrived back in New York with shooting scheduled for early Monday morning. We were going to begin rehearsals that night. Willem told me he would take her out for sushi first to break the ice and they would come by later. Well when later turned to midnight I figured I'd better go to sleep. Willem eventually called saying, "Everything is all right, we will rehearse tomorrow night." Then he added, "But don't call her." Next night same thing, only Willem didn't even bother calling. I was in my apartment late Sunday night, ready to go to sleep, thinking about the next day's shoot with that feel-good, it's-too-late-now excitement, when the doorbell rang. It was Asia. She came in carrying her suitcase, all pissed off, ranting about Willem and the rest of the world. She walked right into my bedroom and started unpacking her bag and putting her things into my chest of drawers. She was still talking when she went into the bathroom and closed the door. I had not moved from my living room chair, watching this like a stage play. I heard the shower running then got a brief glimpse of her as she came back into the bedroom, turned off the lamp, and got under the covers. Call time was 6 a.m.

The most important thing in a relationship with an actor is complete honesty. But I couldn't work up the courage to tell Willem what was going on with me and Asia. Willem was crazy for her. All during the workday, from call in the morning, she maintained the role of Sandii, Willem's muse and lover. But the minute we called wrap she would disappear. I confided in Kelsch and my writer Christ Zois. I told them I needed to tell Willem, I couldn't go on like this. They told me the same thing Asia told me, don't do it, the dailies were too good to risk blowing everything up.

We had a three-day break in the shoot and I booked a hotel suite for Asia and me. We watched Scorcese's

Casino in bed together. Bliss. I fell asleep for an hour and when I woke up she was gone. She had taken the roses I bought her, peeled off the petals, and left a trail of them from the bed down to the floor, all the way to the front door. Later in life she told me it's only when she starts to fall in love with a guy that she begins to serial cheat on him. We went back to work the next day, and all that week she was aloof to me on set or wasn't scheduled. The weekend came and still I didn't hear from her. The weekend is for rehearsals, under normal circumstances, and we had some big stuff coming up. But I wouldn't think of calling Willem. I let it go.

Sunday night around midnight, with another 6 a.m. Monday crew call for both of us, the phone rings. It's her, she's in the apartment the production had rented for her, telling me if I don't come right now she's going to kill herself. I had just scored for the next day and didn't have one fucking penny left on me. It was pouring rain. I walked from way West 26th Street to where we put her up in the West Village. I get inside and she's raving, running through a litany of my offenses. Feeling the lack of a proper response, she takes an envelope off the table. "You know what this is?" I knew what it was, her $1,500 in expense money, fifteen $100 bills given to her in cash each week by the production. She took out one bill calmly and sent it floating down the air shaft of the tiny kitchen window, seven floors down into god knows where. It took me till the third one to come to life and spring for the envelope. She must have been turning toward me at the same time, and I know what you're thinking, tell it to the judge. I didn't mean to hit her, I was trying to close the window, but now blood is running down her nose. She would get these panic attacks where she couldn't breathe, like an asthmatic, and now she's whooping for breath and I'm holding her and trying to stop the bleeding and apologizing, both of us crying. We swore to each other all was ok, we would keep this between us and go to work tomorrow and continue making a great film.

The next day she called her father and told him I punched her like Mike Tyson. The girl is full of these pleasant surprises. As the daughter of a director, and a good director in her own right, she knows how to keep the world on its toes. I had not met her father, but judging by his films and what I would do if one of my daughters had told me this, I was expecting a Sicilian hit man to jump out from behind the next lamppost.

After weeks of Asia insisting that we say nothing to Willem, she spent one lunch hour in his dressing room admitting the whole affair. Blessed Willem took it all in stride and it ended up becoming another building block in our newfound friendship.

We saved the sex scene for last. It is always called the sex scene, and the way it worked is the sound person and Kelsch, the camera in his hands, went into a closed-off room. I was outside with the rest of the crew, watching on a monitor. Somebody says action and it's off to the races. We were shooting film, so the magazine had a ten-and-a-half-minute load before it ran out. The sound of the last inch of film running through the gate was our cut. I am watching the screen and my crew, some of whom I've known my whole life, are watching me, everyone knowing what's going on. I thought I could handle it but I couldn't. At the three-minute mark I just walked away, thinking fuck this movie, fuck the both of them, fuck fuck fuck. She came out in her robe to applause, because those were ten minutes for the books. I looked inside and Kenny, glassy-eyed from looking through the camera that long, gave me a thumbs-up. Willem asked professionally if I needed another take. Yeah, sure. I went to her dressing room and got right in her face. "How could you do that to me?"

"But I did it for you," she said. "I did it for your movie."

This was the movie where shit really fell apart, so when the producers came to me in a panic saying there were a bunch of Jersey state troopers at my DP's house at six in the morning, that seemed normal. Besides, they weren't there to arrest Kenny, they were there to take his guns away from him. It was a nice gesture by some of his Viet vet friends who were on the force, in case he decided to do anything stupid. The divorce he was going through, after eight years of sobriety, was tearing him up. Shooting a feature film was not the first thing on his mind.

Another morning, when we should have been discussing shots like normal directors and DPs, he opened a bag and pulled out a pair of black leather pants. "You know what these are?" Yeah, I knew what they were, I was there when he bought them for Dale ten years earlier with the last money he had, the one thing she really wanted. What made him late was he used his special forces training to break into her new boyfriend's house, where she and the kids were now living, and while everyone was asleep stole the pants and left unnoticed. "What if the boyfriend caught you?" I asked. He answered with that crazy smile of his.

Steve Drellich, the second cameraman, stepped up and was shooting while Kenny was on the phone battling with the divorce lawyers. Drellich is a cool cameraman, but he was constantly stopping and asking to check a shadow in the background or something only he could see and I could give a fuck about. Not to put him down, but nobody shoots like Kenny. Kenny doesn't frame actors, he takes a bead on them like a sniper waiting to pull the trigger.

By the time shooting ended, my paranoid, out-of-control behavior had led to a split-up with my longtime composer Joe Delia and my editor Tony Redman, two dear friends. I was alone, broken, with everyone thinking we had not shot enough scenes. I was in the production office when my producer Jay Cannold, a quiet and unassuming dude, handed me a document laying out various rehabs, where they were and how I could get into them. A spiritual offering if there ever was one. I looked at it, incredulous. Was this for me? I didn't need this, I just needed ten dollars from him for a bag of dope to get me back on my feet. Not some overpriced mental institution my DGA insurance would have paid for. Movie directors have one of the few insurance plans that provide for that.

When Tony and I split up, his young assistant Jim, the brother of our actress Gretchen Mol, took over. He went mad for Asia. He had never met her but the process of going through the footage over and over, fast and slow, backwards, freezing individual frames, did it to him. The whole edit started to shift to her. He would sneak into the editing room after-hours and start changing an agreed-upon sequence. He was mirroring Dafoe's character, whose obsession with Sandii in the story ends up getting him and everyone else killed.

Asia came back to New York for some pickup shooting at the end of the editing, but she was dealing with me at arm's length. I wanted her to stay with me but she said she was staying with friends. Then I got a call from someone telling me my girlfriend had moved in with the Wu-Tang Clan. I told him he was crazy, but how would I know where she was.

The day of the re-shoots I was with one camera

crew outside, filming desolate night streets, while Kenny was inside shooting her stuff. When I got back I thought a party was going on. Asia was straddling Kelsch, who was holding the camera getting a POV of her face for the sex scene, she and the crew laughing and having a ball, me in the doorway at the other end of the loft, miserable.

She said she was leaving for Tokyo from LaGuardia at midnight, and would be gone for a week or so to work on a script with someone important there. She promised that when she got back we would be together. I decided to go for it all and buy her an engagement ring and propose to her before the plane left. You can't blame this kind of delusional thinking on drugs and alcohol. You have to take your basic character into consideration.

I went over to the Chelsea Hotel, room 914, to see Franky, my drug dealer. When his customers didn't have money for drugs he would accept all kinds of things, guitars, cameras, computers. He had an eyepiece and knew how to use it, so he had a nice collection of jewelry too. He fronted me the ring I wanted, but by the time we finished getting high and making the deal her plane had long left. I promised myself I would be on the runway when she got back with the thousand-dollar diamond. Then, like the dealer, psychiatrist, and friend he was, Franky said, "Planes don't leave for Tokyo from LaGuardia." Way later I discovered she did take a plane from LaGuardia, to Buffalo with Vinny Gallo for the premiere of *Buffalo '66*, where he introduced her to his parents before they all went to his opening together.

Asia is in recovery with me now, and when I get into those dark, evil states of mind, and I don't need the drugs or alcohol to get there, she's one of the people I reach out to. Like her performances in the films, she has never let me down, not for one frame. She finds the right words and the right way to say them to get me through.

BUSTED 3

I was living with Marla, or she was staying in my apartment was more like it. We had broken up a while ago, but whenever she needed a place to stay she would ask and I would never say no. I was still hopelessly in love with her. Carrying a torch is a soulless occupation. I would profess my undying love, but when I used the word "us" she would say matter-of-factly, "But there is no us anymore."

It was New Year's Eve, a scary night for an everyday drinker having to maneuver around a city full of drunks. I was working with Walken on something, and he suggested we have dinner at his house and rehearse for a while. I was planning on spending it at Nancy's apartment with some of our drug dealer friends, but Marla hadn't seen Chris in a long time and wanted to go. I thought he would be at his apartment up near the Museum of Natural History, but at the last minute he told me he was at his house in Connecticut. Fuck, who wanted to be driving to Connecticut on New Year's Eve. Off we went, but by the time we got there Walken was already loaded. He was watching Mel Gibson's new film *Braveheart*, a tape he received from the Academy for voting purposes. Across the bottom of the screen was the FBI warning against illegal copying. After a while Chris asked, "Why are there subtitles if the film is in English?" Rehearsing was out the window.

I was stuck at the dinner table with Walken's wife Georgianne, a very good casting agent but someone who could drive me crazy, Chris, who was done for the evening, and Marla. I stood up to go to the bathroom, walked out the front door and into my brand-new Jeep, no goodbye, no nothing, and took off back to NYC and the drug party at my house.

I was feeling free, Creedence on the tape deck, the moon out, the cool old tree-lined Merritt Parkway empty of cars, a new year about to begin, when I heard the siren and saw the flashing lights. I'd had a few beers but was cogent when the young nervous Connecticut trooper went through the license and registration ritual. He asked if I knew I was driving past the speed limit, way past, and if I had had anything to drink. I looked him straight in the eye and told him I never had a drink in my life and I was driving fast because my wife was having our baby at any moment and I needed to get there. He wanted to know why I smelled like beer, then went through the walk-a-straight-line and a few other tests, all the while saying, "Don't get too close to me." He held up my license and said, "This is an expired California license. Are you aware of that?" I said no. He said, "I'll keep this," and went back to his car and left. I couldn't believe it. I drove off thinking I'd witnessed the first miracle of what I was sure was going to be my year. Back to singing "Lodi," but five minutes down the highway, on the New York border, was a massive traffic stop, cops all over, lights and sirens. I was trapped in a line of cars waiting to be grilled by New York police officers. The state trooper had known what he was doing. He called ahead and figured let them handle it. They were waiting for me. When I got up to the front of the line they just opened my door and said, "Abel, get out." Two guys held me and before I could come up with some bullshit, one of them stuck a straw in my mouth and I blew a DUI. They had tractor trailers set up on the edge of the highway with makeshift cells. Inside, a cop at a desk asked me a bunch of questions, including, "What's your mother's maiden name?"

"O'Brien," as if that had anything to with anything. He led me to a chair facing the camera and asked me to hold up a number for the mugshot. They were hootin' and hollerin' outside as it turned to midnight. That was the beginning of my year.

They put me in a cell with two young Black dudes and we just waited. After a while they brought in a big tall dashiki'd-out middle-aged African guy who started screaming to see someone in charge, saying there had been some mistake, that he was a diplomat from Zimbabwe and that they had no right to hold him here and on and on. Outside was the sound of firecrackers. One of the cops came over and told him, "Calm down, the firing squad is waiting outside." Well the cop's idea of a joke set this dude into a panic. He started pulling at the bars of our temporary cell, shaking the whole trailer. Me and the two brothers were crouched in the corner. Finally, in desperation, I said to him, "I know it don't look like it, but I have a lot of influence around here. As soon as I get out I'll get someone from the embassy to come help you."

Eventually they let us out and told me my car had been towed and there were livery drivers on their way. Oh really? I had five bucks in my pocket. I walked outside in the freezing cold, no jacket because that was in the car, and now I remembered so was Marla's computer, all on their way to a gas station in Port Chester somewhere.

None of the drivers wanted to hear about credit. Finally a woman with an Irish accent heard me out. "I need to get home to my wife and kids but I'll have to go upstairs and get the money once we get there." Like a saint she let me in, and talked about Ireland the whole ride into the city. When we got there I went upstairs, but nobody had arrived yet and Nancy had no money, so I invited the woman up to my apartment, where she sat content until someone showed up who could pay her.

’R XMAS

New Rose played at Venice to some good reviews and mostly-confused audiences. It didn’t help that Pressman said at the press conference that the film was a work in progress, which it wasn’t. The domestic release was another disaster. I was disconnected from my filmmaking family, and my actual family, plunging deeper into the day-to-day necessity of heroin addiction. If you’re not being sick you’re getting sick. Dealers become your life and you delude yourself into thinking they’re your friends. Nicky was gone. I was looking for a project. I was yearning to do a documentary but I didn’t know it yet. Scripts bored me, stories bored me, all of them seemed so lame. My past movies seemed preposterous, made up. Then one night I was with Annabella Sciorra when we met this Puerto Rican woman named Cassandra, a heroin dealer from Washington Heights. She told me her story, which was exactly what I had been looking for, and that's *'R Xmas.*

The event took place in 1993, the height of the pre-Giuliani laissez-faire attitude toward drug enforcement, a liberal Black mayor, David Dinkins, in charge. If there was a war on drugs the outlaws were winning. But this holiday season the cops in that hood had had enough of revolving-door justice and went renegade on some of the local dealers.

Cassandra was married to a mild-mannered, small-time young street dealer whose boss was an old man with one solid South American heroin connection. The shit arrived once a month, sometimes in a box of shoes. He was instructed to go to a certain store and request a certain style and size. The next month it might be to a bakery to request a certain kind of cake. It was a small, steady business that earned the old man 100k a month, tax free. When he knew he was dying he left the whole business to the young husband because he liked him. The kid was out of his depth, with nowhere near what it takes to run an operation like that, but Cassandra, his wife, did. She was a natural-born drug boss.

They had two spots, an out-of-the-way housing project in the Bronx and a side street in Spanish Harlem. They would bag up the shit in her uncle's apartment on the third floor of a nondescript building in Washington Heights. Her other uncle had a small car service in the neighborhood and he would deliver to the two spots. It was a small, self-contained enterprise, and after a couple of years, well, multiply 24 by 100,000.

Like any upwardly mobile NYC executive, she wanted up and out of Washington Heights. They found a nice duplex in a ritzy apartment in a good neighborhood in the Bronx, a state-of-the art Mercedes, designer clothes, and private schools in Manhattan for her seven- and ten-year-olds. Life was great until the cops, fed up with watching all of this, came down on the husband and a few other dealers in the neighborhood two days before Christmas. The guy got grabbed, blindfolded, and brought to a place underneath the West Side Highway. They laid him on the ground and fired a burst from some confiscated Uzi close enough to his head to scare the shit out of him forever. Then they tied him up and threw him under a pool table in one of the cop's rec rooms while the leader of the group went to inform Cassandra of the news. He told her it would cost her 150k in cash to get him back. She played dumb, acting like she didn't have the money. He gave her until midnight Christmas Eve to deliver or else. Like some of my female partners, she didn't think hers was worth 150k. She basically said fuck him, but his boys and family convinced her it was just the price of doing business, and she reluctantly bought him back. He showed up alive Christmas morning in time for the kids to open their presents under the tree in their big beautiful apartment, with a message that if they ever saw him on the street selling anything again they would kill him. Whether Cassandra believed him or not, she was definitely not giving up her lifestyle to move back in with her mother in Washington Heights. "And what are you going to do if you stop dealing?" she asked him. "Work at McDonald's?"

"Why not?" If you've seen the movie you know the ending. If you haven't, go find a copy. Good luck with that.

The film starred Drea de Matteo and Lillo Brancato. Lillo was discovered off the streets of Yonkers as a teenager to play De Niro's son in *Bronx Tale.* He was originally from Colombia, adopted by Italian parents. He effortlessly captured the innocence of the Dominican street dealer, more a victim of circumstance than a born street thug. Drea had a Spanish background too and could speak the language. She shined as the powerful matriarch of this unlikely drug crew. Lillo was suffering psychologically and was using drugs, only I didn't know it. He was physically withdrawing during an important scene, which is funny because I had the shit he needed right in my pocket, if only we were communicating our addictions.

The film drove me even deeper into the drug world. Nancy was in the same place, and although I was financially keeping it together most of the time, I was a failure as a father. I was delusional, thinking as long as I'm earning money and paying the bills

I'm covered. The real delusion was thinking the drugs were helping me accomplish this.

Today I can make amends to my daughter Endira, and living amends to both of them, but Lucy does not speak to me or her mother. I can understand why. I can only hope one day that will change.

Soon after the film played in Cannes, Lillo was tried and convicted as an accomplice in the killing of a cop. He got ten years in prison. The police were not happy with that sentence. They filled the courtroom, demanding blood. Who could blame them?

The story I got was Lillo and the father of Lillo's seventeen-year-old girlfriend were out partying in Manhattan. Go-go joints were Lillo's thing. He was a tough dude but not as tough as he thought. The father, who kept a 9mm under his dashboard for company, was.

Somewhere where the Bronx meets Westchester there lived a Viet vet who dealt out of a stand-alone two-story house on a block full of them. He had died of natural causes six months earlier, so the house stood empty. Every one of his clients, Lillo included, had broken in countless times, tearing up the floorboards, smashing in the walls, digging holes in the cellar, hoping to find some hidden stash that was long gone if it ever existed. At five in the morning, tweaking and hurting and not getting through to their normal connects, Lillo and the father went back to the empty house to try again. Lillo, wiry and athletic, climbed through a window but shattered some glass doing it, waking an off-duty police officer who lived a few doors down. The officer got up and, wearing only jeans and a T-shirt and his weapon, went to investigate. Lillo's friend, who was convicted of pulling the trigger, had no idea he was killing a cop. The karma for the death of that dedicated officer is not only on him, it's on all of us users, for the abuse of alcohol and drugs, the desperate and endless need for them.

EVICTION

ITALY

If you have never gotten evicted from your apartment I would suggest you pay your rent or leave voluntarily. I was $30,000 behind on mine, back living with Nancy and the kids. It was exactly seven o'clock in the morning when we heard the knock I knew was coming. The landlord arrived with the marshal, a mean-looking fifty-something white guy with a pistol in his holster and his ID looped around his neck. Nancy pleaded with him. He didn't want to hear shit. We were out in the street. Lucy wasn't the kind of kid who cried a lot, but she was crying that morning as we all stood on the corner of Christopher and Washington Streets just off the West Side Highway, me dopesick next to my wife, also dopesick, not a dime on us.

I reached out to a crew member of mine, who luckily was home, and she gave me enough money to score while Nancy and Lucy waited out of the rain in a breakfast place nearby. Another friend's wife, out of the kindness of her heart, came through with a couple of nights at the Chelsea Hotel. At 3 p.m. we needed to get Endira from the Little Red School House. I can only imagine how she felt when we picked her up, having no idea when she left for school that morning that she would never see her bedroom and all her things in it again. That's not something you do to a twelve-year-old. But that's where that life takes you and everyone close to you, right into the gutter.

I was good at borrowing 20s and 50s, but not good at asking for more. I hadn't talked to Chris Walken in a few years. I called him at home. "Chris?"

"Oh Abel, oh hi?"

"Chris can you lend me ten thousand dollars?"

"Yes, sure." Simple as that when you have generous and beautiful friends. I got us a nice apartment way up on 107th Street, right off Central Park West. Nancy and the kids liked it a lot. They had the park right there. I was far from my downtown scene and getting a different perspective on the city. The Trade Towers were gone. In their place was a whole new Manhattan, a safe haven for every hedge fund hustler and international rip-off artist driving the average New Yorker from his home or business. To top it off the broken window policy was in place, and so was stop and frisk, right out of the Hitler handbook. So if you jumped a turnstile you had more of a chance of being picked up and booked than if you thieved a million-dollar stock deal on Wall Street.

Producers have always been afraid to come and shoot in NYC, but the terrorist threat gave them an extra reason to buy into that bullshit that Toronto or Detroit or Montreal look just like New York. Really? I wasn't about to go back to LA, and no one was offering me anything there anyway, especially not for the films I wanted to make. Then out of the blue I got an offer to go to Italy to finance the script I was working on. I was back sitting in the front of the plane, drinking Barolo, dreaming big dreams on the night flight to Rome. As Nicky D used to say, "Back on top."

JERUSALEM

JULIETTE

Jerusalem was a turning point. If you have never been, go. The clay that the buildings are made of gives off this incredible pink glow when the sun sets. *Mary* was a film within a film about Mary Magdalene and her relationship to Jesus Christ. The producers talked about Morocco, where Scorsese shot *Last Temptation*. I was taken to Matera in Italy, where Mel Gibson and Pasolini shot their crucifixion scenes. Naturally no one said, "Let's go to Jerusalem, where it really happened," but that's where I went. I knew if I was to make a film about who Mary Magdalene really was, it had to be there.

The first bit of intel is that they didn't crucify Jesus on a hill outside the city, but at the entrance coming into it. It was done as a warning to the country people arriving for Passover, to say, have a nice holiday with your families, but if you think you're going to start robbing the place or talking shit against the state, here's what happens. Pound you naked into a board and leave you there for a few days.

Stand at the final station of the cross and you are in a bazaar, surrounded by nonbelievers, the Muslims and the Jews selling rock 'n' roll T-shirts, DVDs, rugs, and trinkets to pilgrims from all over the world who are being led Disneyland-style through all of it. Still it's a powerful spot, and right there my journey toward getting straight, getting some real spiritual healing, began. I felt Him. Like Marley sings, "Almighty God is a living man." Christ as the good son, Christ as rebel, martyr to the oppressive political system of both the Romans and the Pharisees. Christ the simple rabbi with the Magdalene as his wife. Take a real look at Da Vinci's *Last Supper* and there she is right in front of you. I had seen that painting so many times, but always from inside the box I was put in to believe no woman was worthy of sitting at that table.

The Buddhist practice says the source of all wisdom is the female, so you better connect with one or find the female inside yourself. The legacy of Mary Magdalene through the years, from the wife to the whore, then to oblivion, is the Church's denial of the female. Mary's gospel, her testament of love and brilliance contained in the Dead Sea Scrolls, was desecrated and denied. Why? Maybe if you cut the women out there's more money for the rest of us men to split around those long tables.

This was a film for Lucy and Endira, adopted from Mother Teresa's orphanage in Calcutta. Being of color and a woman is two strikes against you before you even get to the plate. We were driving down Broadway at Houston Street one day and there was a giant ad featuring a teen model plastered on the side of a building. Someone in the car said to Lucy, who was four at the time, "Would you like to model someday?" She said, "They don't put brown people in those pictures." She got it. Whether Jesus was brown, who knows. He certainly wasn't lily-white, because Sephardic Jews and Arabs share the same skin color, which is the first thing you notice when you get there.

Fernando Sulichin is from Argentina. I met him soon after he came to NYC, when he brought Lily Taylor up to the loft to introduce her to us for *The Addiction.* I could see he was the kind of boots-on-the-ground producer who fit right in with us, a stone hustler. He went on to get future secretary of state Anthony Blinken to invest money in the project, and years later delivered Putin and Castro for Oliver Stone's two brilliant documentaries. So when I was financing *Mary*, struggling to bring my new band of Bolognese gangster investors, cash-rich from handmaking rip-off Pradas and Armanis, into business with Vincent Maraval and the Wild Bunch, I called Fernando. Somehow he managed to balance those two crews, the Italian ministry, and us, a three-language parlay.

Now it hinged on who would play Mary. Juliette Binoche was up for a meeting. I flew to Paris just for the day because we didn't have enough money for a hotel. I would meet her at the restaurant atop the Pompidou while Fernando waited at a bar nearby. When I arrived they sat me at a corner table with a nice bottle of wine, saying Ms. Binoche would arrive shortly.

I sat, waiting and drinking. After an hour they came by to tell me she would be a bit late, something about picking up her kids at school. Another hour went by. I called Fernando and said, "I'm leaving, fuck the bitch." He begged me to give her another half hour, so I waited. After god knows how much drinking and how many trips to the bathroom to stay high, the staff had changed shifts and had started cleaning up. The new waiter said they were getting ready to close, and that I had to leave. I told him I was waiting for Juliette Binoche. He looked at me like I was crazy and said, "Get out of here before we call the cops." At that moment Juliette sailed into the room, apologized briefly to everyone, and sat down. The waiter asked what she would like to drink. No one was going home until she left.

She took out the script and opened it, and all I could see were redlines, highlights, and comments. Even the backs of the pages were covered in her notes. She told me she had been planning on doing a film on Magdalene for five years, but that the project had fallen through. I felt the tables turning. I was no longer auditioning her as an actress, she was auditioning me as a director. She began talking about the Gospel of Mary and Mary's true relationship to Jesus Christ. We were soul brother and sister on all of it. The meeting ended and we had our lead.

I had to get to the airport to make the last flight, but Fernando insisted we stop at a bar to see a young actress who could be good for the movie. I wanted no part of it, there wasn't time. But ten minutes later he had the taxi cab pull up to a bar and inside I was introduced to Marion Cotillard. She was just beginning her career, spoke zero English, but who cared. The meeting lasted thirty seconds. She got the job, and I made my plane.

SHANYN

MULBERRY STREET

We won the Jury Prize in Venice with *Mary* and I came back to NYC to prep the prequel to *King of New York*, but at this point I was too fucked up to pull off an undertaking like that. My crew were all in recovery, so they were the last people I wanted to be around. I was downtown, only on the West Side now, an apartment on Sullivan Street surrounded by dealers, addicts, and West Side mafiosi. I was living with Shanyn, who didn't drink or get high, so we were together in name and place only, our lives as separate as possible under the guise of a director/actress relationship. Her day-to-day activities were yoga classes, veganism, and a meditation group. I dabbled in the first two, but the Buddhist classes I hit seriously. They were making great sense to me. Her teacher Phuntsok, born in Haiti, who studied with the Dalai Lama in Dharamshala, was giving me the Middle Way right from the source. I read the books but more importantly I had them explained to me line by line in the classes, the only way to get it. I meditated, went to retreats, and became a follower of Lama Yeshe, who had died in the early '70s, so all you have are some YouTube teachings and his books, but that's plenty. The part of the teaching I missed was it doesn't work if you're fucked up. You can't snort some dope and think you are having a powerful meditation, even if you are on the most spiritual of retreats. It only works when it's for others, to make yourself more capable of being of service to those around you. It can't be self-centered, and a drug addict is the most selfish person in the world. You're not on earth to suffer, says the Buddha. If you're suffering you're seeing the world in a delusional state. Not hit by a car or felled by a horrible disease kind of suffering, the self-inflicted kind.

Like a lot of my exes, Shanyn could write a book of her exploits between seventeen and twenty-one years old, but they rarely tell those stories. It began for her as a teenager, skipping high school and taking the bus into Manhattan from her family home in New Jersey. She hooked up to one of those Gypsy women who would hang their shingle on West 3rd Street, and like Franky C said, "Once those Gypsies got their hooks in you, it's all over." The Gypsy did a ritual with blood and an egg and an embryo, and after that she had Shanyn hustling guys for their credit cards, which the Gypsy would take to Toys "R" Us with her four kids.

Ray, a dear friend of mine, was one of the credit card givers and that's how I met her. She was a talented actress with a special spirit and beautiful long red hair. Our relationship began in Rome when I was shooting *Mary* and continued till I got sober. She gave a strong performance in *Go Go Tales* and killed it in *4:44*. All the while the Gypsy was a third party in our relationship, controlling Shanyn's decisions and taking plenty of money for it.

We moved to Franky C's apartment above the La Mela restaurant on Mulberry near Broome. They would start cooking tomato sauce early in the morning and I would wake up to the smell of garlic. For me it was confirmation that we were going to eat that day, but Shanyn hated that smell and hated the street and the people, and probably me too at that point. Franky C's office was across the hall. On his wall were pieces of paper with the names and numbers of people who borrowed money from him. I was one of the boys, so I could borrow what I wanted with no interest, as long as I gave it back. Franky would say, "There's plenty of room on that wall." I was living rent free but paying for it with the guilt trip he would lay on me, because that's how these guys operate. In that world it's psychological warfare 24/7. Being chill is not in the Italian American gangster program.

By then Bud Light was my drink of choice. It had

to be cold and in the 22 oz glass bottles, because a guy who worked at the Budweiser factory across the river in Jersey told me they made those with the most care. I am the kind of person who not only believes bullshit like that but gets obsessive about it.

The new drug score back then was at 6:15 in the morning on Mulberry between Houston and Prince, around the corner from the methadone clinic. I told Shanyn I was turning over a new leaf and starting work early in the morning, when I worked best. The addicts with any cash would arrive and wait for this crazy Spanish dude who came in from Queens. The deal with the cops was that as long as everyone was gone by 7 a.m., when the mothers started walking their kids to school, everyone could get hooked up. This was the working man's spot, guys who needed their fix to make it to their 9 to 5. There would be mailmen in uniforms, Wall Street guys in suits, all kinds of regular people mixed in with the career zombies. He would also have the coke, so I was fine till 12:30, my real hookup on 26th Street. Even though money was a big problem, Shanyn had no idea I was spending $200 a day to support my habit.

Franky C died of colon cancer. Soon after there was a knock on my door. In walks Carmine, a guy I knew had just come out of jail. After some small talk across my little kitchen table he said, "Not for nothing, but are you ever going to pay me my rent?" I'm looking at this dude thinking, Franky has been torturing me over this place for two and a half years and it didn't even belong to him? I'm good with numbers, but at $2,500 a month there was no point in computing that. I said, "You need all the back rent, now?"

"Never mind the back rent, just start paying me this month, ok?"

"Fine." I'm walking down Mulberry Street to my office, which was the bar at Marcello's Restaurant between Grand and Hester, whose cash register was my ATM machine. Marcello's used to be John Gotti's restaurant and you can still feel his vibe, especially down in the cellar where we put together an editing room. Who knows what was behind those stone walls. Sitting at the bar, listening to the piano player, my drug dealer, who I'd convinced Marcello to hire, now I'm cool with the world.

Whether it was the AA meetings I was sporadically attending or a desire to lose weight, or divine intervention, one day I stopped drinking. And, for the first time, I kept my drug use hidden. I would go to the Midnite Group on Houston Street and lie about how many days clean I had, then get high in the bathroom of the meeting, which in a room full of people fighting for their lives is about as low as you can go. I made my amends to that group years later, and they just laughed and got a big kick out of it.

WELCOME TO NEW YORK

It was the spring of 2011 when Dominique Strauss-Kahn got in trouble with the law in NYC. I got the full brunt of the media splurge. You have to go a long way to take over the cover of the *New York Post* for a month, but if you are about to be the next president of France and are accused of carrying a 6 foot, 200 lb African cleaning woman down the hall and raping her in your Midtown hotel room, that will do it. Nafissatou Diallo was her name, from Guinea. The case played out over the summer, ending one day in August with her close-up on the front page, the word "hooker" printed over it. That cover supposedly cost DSK's wife Anne Sinclair two million dollars to run. The DA dropped the case and the rest of New York moved on. Sinclair eventually paid another two million to Diallo and her lawyer as a final settlement. Like the rape of the nuns back in the '80s that triggered *Bad Lieutenant*, this is a story that sticks with you.

Vincent Maraval ran Wild Bunch, a rock 'em sock 'em shoot-from-the-hip company based out of Paris that financed, produced, and distributed movies. We had been doing business together for more than ten years. The company was named more for a lifestyle than for Peckinpah's great film, and we all did our best to live up to Sam and the company name. Vincent had listened to my crazy scheme of producing *4:44* for a half a million dollars, Dafoe getting a third, me and the crew getting a third, and the financiers the other third, splitting the money earned from dollar one. Sounds fair, but nobody but Vincent would have agreed to it.

He would always come to the set one day during a shoot, as much for good luck as anything else, and this was the day. We wrapped at five in the morning and he and I and Peter Danner, a financial partner of ours, walked through Chinatown, dodging some impressive-looking rats before settling into my usual hangout, a 7-Eleven-styled all-night deli on the corner of Broome and Centre Streets. We sat at the counter, staring out the storefront window, drinking coffee out of Styrofoam cups and kicking shit around, when the Strauss-Kahn case came up. Maraval's eyes lit up and he threw out Depardieu for the lead with Isabelle Adjani for the wife. My experience with Vincent is he doesn't talk shit he can't deliver, so I'm thinking, wow, we got the next picture financed before we even finished shooting this one. I should have known better.

Cut to a year later and I am back to being broke on my ass, still living above La Mela on Mulberry Street, when Vincent calls saying we need to see Depardieu right away with the script. We didn't have one, but they had already booked flights for me, Shanyn, Christ Zois, and his girlfriend. Christ, or Chris, is a psychiatrist, the screenwriter of *New Rose Hotel* and *The Blackout,* and confidant to many of my later films. He put something together quick while I dove into researching the subject, my favorite part of the process.

We arrived in Paris after an all-night flight and headed directly to Gérard's house. He lives in a palatial mansion, which is the only way to describe it, in the 6th arrondissement, surrounded by high walls. He also owns the restaurant across the street. We rolled in on him around nine in the morning. Maraval, his people, and my group entered a party already in full swing. The magnum of champagne that Depardieu opened had his profile burned into the top of the cork, because he owns the vineyard too. The chef brought in a freshly killed lamb he was about to cook and was showing it off in front of my vegan crew. It all had the feel of a film that's about to happen. The script conversation between Zois and Gérard was more *King Lear* than the actual event, but who cared.

I made it back to our hotel with visions of the filming and was getting ready to meet Isabelle Adjani. It would have been too convenient for her to have come to Gérard's, instead she wanted to meet that afternoon at my hotel, which she then proceeded to cancel. They changed the meeting to the next morning and moved our flight a day later. All well and good, only I didn't bring enough dope to make it that far, and Paris is not a place for a one-day visitor to cop in a foreign language. And with heroin, unlike coke, it's not proper film business etiquette to ask the production to help you score.

They say a junkie keeps his stash right next to his balls, which in my case was the tiny pocket on the right side of my jeans, which is why I wore them religiously. It was 100 percent the law, formal wear was a tux jacket and black wranglers with the shit safe and sound, right on your hip. This night for some reason I put half my meager stash in the hotel safe. Thank god, because when I woke up the next morning in my usual way, reaching in my pocket as I opened my eyes, I found nothing inside the folded bill but a little note saying, "God is watching you." Every once in a while Shanyn would try to help bring me back to earth by pulling shit like this, flushing what I had down the toilet.

We met Isabelle, and she needed Zois the psychiatrist more than Abel the director. Instead of talking about Anne Sinclair, the character she was playing, she spent the whole time crying over her guy Daniel Day-Lewis, sharing a lot of things she should have kept between the two of them as I got sicker and sicker, the need a ticking time bomb inside my body, a steady progression into agony. The smack, the dooj, the babanya, as the mob guys call it. I was sixteen years into daily use. Read Bulgakov's "Morphine." I managed, like many times before, to tough it through an extra night and a brutal plane ride home. The piano player was waiting for me in the lobby of my building.

REHAB

Ray was a superstar white basketball player from Jersey who played at Georgia Tech on his way to pro ball in South America. He ran a hip diner in South Beach in Miami, but was also in the construction business in Virginia. He had a partner named James and together they were building a shopping center in the suburbs outside of DC, with all the political connections you need for something like that. James lived there with his wife and two loving teenage children. He kept his hair short and was buttoned-down for business reasons, but he could go gangster in a hurry. He had another life, centered around an apartment he kept near the Newark airport, with a manic stewardess that came with it, doing all the dope and coke and Xanax they could get their hands on. I introduced James to our dealer Javi and he was forever grateful to me, saying it was the best introduction he ever had. Javi would overnight him packages to Virginia whenever he ran out of stuff, or meet him at the Newark airport when he arrived hurting.

Around 4:30 one morning I got a text from Ray in Miami saying, "Get over to Newark right away." I was still trying to figure out how I was going to do that when I got a another one, fifteen minutes later, saying, "Too late." James had written his last text message, asking Ray to stay close to his son and daughter. Then he picked up a Glock someone had bought him for Christmas and blew his brains out. While mourning his death, Javi, who didn't provide Xanax or advocate its use, told me, "If he would've stayed off the X and stuck to the dope and the coke, none of this would have happened."

Six months later, on a beautiful spring day, I'm walking down my favorite street in NYC, 26th west of Broadway, the heart of the Flower District, where my dealer lives. She's Javi's sister-in-law, a Colombian ex-dancer, a young, on-the-rise businesswoman. She was always home and always had the best shit for the best price. Everyone had an appointment time. Mine was 12:30, and that did not mean 12:35. She lived in a little Hansel-and-Gretel-looking five-story building with crooked wooden steps leading up to her apartment. The closer I get to it the better I'm feeling. Then I run into James's daughter, who had just started classes at the Fashion Institute down the block. She's radiant, happy to see me, hugging me, but not a word is spoken of her father, who I know she adored. I have to hold back the tears, telling her, "Now that you're living in New York, make sure you call me for anything, and good luck at school."

You search for the moment, and maybe there is none. The white light experience happens to some, like Bill, member number one of the program. Carl Jung once wrote to him that the worst feeling a doctor can have is when he understands his patient's illness but can offer no cure. He wrote, "'Alcohol' in Latin is 'spiritus' and you use the same word for the highest religious experience as well as for the most depraving poison. The helpful formula therefore is: 'spiritus contra spiritum.'" It can only be cured by a spiritual awakening. In one's darkest moment, an act of grace.

Salvatore is a young actor from Marianella, a rough section of Napoli. He's been in a few of my films and calls me his brother, though the relationship is more father and son. His neighborhood is the epicenter of the European drug trade, but he has never used. He was a boxer on the rise till he punched out a referee during the Olympic trials, got disqualified, and went into the movies full-time. One day he turned to me and said, "I can get you all the drugs in Napoli, but I can also bring you to a place where you can get help, and I will pay for it." It was a sincere offer, one I ignored until the chance meeting with James's daughter on the street.

All that junkies do when they're together is talk about cutting back or quitting altogether, but in America a proper rehab can cost up to 100k a month. What addict has people around him who can pay for that, or still care to? I got lucky.

Salvatore brought me to a place in the mountains above Napoli, situated thirty minutes north of where my grandfather was born and thirty minutes east of where Padre Pio was born. Because Italy is a socialist country, it was government supported. One hundred kids in recovery, mostly eighteen to twenty-five, getting a chance to step off their personal merry-go-rounds, spending their days learning to fix cars or build wooden furniture or grow flowers or whatever. The food they ate they grew. Tony Palma, who ran it, was not a doctor, in fact I think he started life as a beautician, but he had been treating addicts for thirty years and knew what was needed on a practical level. He wasn't about orders, he was about love. He spoke no English. He took me aside, put his arm around my shoulder knowingly, and said, "Vincere," the mantra of Caesar's army. You can win. He knew some of the gangster producers I was associated with, the ones hoping the process wouldn't take more than a week so that I could return to being the catalyst for raising production money. Tony let me know, you have one real friend, Salvatore. The rest, lose. I did, along with everyone else I ever used with.

I didn't stay that day, although I should have. I

still needed another week of torture. I was the special guest of a film festival in Ischia, a magical little island right off the coast, where I was getting some award. Ischia, like all festivals, is basically there to pump up the local tourist trade. Pascal Vicedomini would host it in the summertime, pulling some American stars and whichever big-shot executives were chilling on their yachts in the Mediterranean that summer. It was a nice ride on a private boat to a cool hotel, and all I needed to do was hang out for a bit and get onstage one night and accept an award. This week I was especially fucked up. I had had enough of all the bullshit, the beautiful pool, the beautiful beach, the beautiful afternoon lunches on the beautiful yachts, everything that was being offered to me. When my name got called, Pascal stood onstage alone in front of all the Hollywood dudes and local dignitaries, holding the award, waiting, because I was on the local ferry making a quick run to Napoli to re-up my supply. When he asked me the next morning, with the sweetest look on his face, "How could you do that to me?" I told him I had gotten the days mixed up. The reality was I didn't give a fuck, not about him or his festival or whoever the fuck was there that could possibly help get our next gig.

Shanyn was with me at the festival for the right reasons. She wanted to meet people. The final night one of Tarantino's producers, who I had known in another lifetime, was at the bar and wanted to say hello. Shanyn begged me to go downstairs, and for the sake of peace in the family I went. I didn't even try to make conversation. I stood, shades on, downing a liter or two of San Pellegrino right from the bottle, waiting for the moment I could leave. It all ends the same for every addict, in isolation. After all the bars and parties and the theoretical good times. They call sobriety finding the self of your former ghost. I was in full Jacob Marley mode.

Kenny always says, who is sicker, us or the women who are with us? Shanyn had her own demons, maybe that was the connection. We were way past I'm a director and you're an actress whose career I could help, way beyond that. This was the day she had always hoped would come. I was leaving the island for rehab. I was in the hotel room, shades drawn, dopesick to beat the band, because there was never enough at that point. She was incredibly loving to me in this moment. We checked out of the hotel and made it down to the dock to wait for the noon boat. Gaetano, my crazy Neapolitan producer, came up to me with the bad news, the ferry was an hour late. Then the good news, Fabio, my other producer slash lawyer, will be waiting at the dock for me in Napoli, code for he'll have the shit with him. Then Gaetano and his girl and my girl went off to have a pleasant lunch at the local pizzeria like normal people, while I just lay down on the bench above the metal grating of the dock, in the blazing sun, waiting for the boat. Neapolitans like to talk loud, and the sound of voices when you are jonesing is like a razor blade going through your inner ear. As the dock filled with people the noise got louder, echoing through the grating. Why would an otherwise healthy person put himself through this? "Why do you continue to poison yourself?" Kenny used to ask me in frustration. Thankfully I was on my way to finding the answers to that question.

I got off the boat ride from hell, which was a pleasant forty-five-minute sail across the Mediterranean for everyone else, and there was my friend, my lawyer, who I would never see again, waiting. We hugged and kissed South Italy style, which is perfect cover for the half a gram he slipped me. Just feeling the bag in my hand took my pain away. The addiction to heroin is physical but the psychological side is immense. Knowing I had it made me well, but not as well as snorting it there in the cafe, in one of my favorite bathrooms in the world, on the same dock where my grandfather left for America a zillion years ago. My last hit of drugs.

They gave me methadone the first night, 50 milligrams, then 45 the next day, then 40, then 35, and after ten days I was off everything. Then you're on your own. My room overlooked a chicken coop next to the farmhouse. The electricity was turned off for everyone else at 10 p.m., but I had an electric lamp because of my VIP status. No internet or phone. In the next two months, in the heat of that South Italian summer, I don't think I slept more than ten minutes at a time, day or night. I thought and I read. I went and got books by the pound, subject, author, who cared? The bigger the better. I read *Moby-Dick*. How they expected me to understand that book as a teenager I have no idea, but I got it now. Melville spending page after page explaining how to tie a sailor's knot was fine with me. *Dracula* and *Frankenstein*, Mailer's *Harlot's Ghost*, Tolstoy.

Poe started not working for me, Burroughs neither. I was feeling the drugs and alcohol in the writing I once adored, and was uncomfortable with it, like when Hemingway trashed Faulkner, saying he knew at what line in the story he took his first drink. I read one of Poe's letters to a friend asking for help to start a literary journal. He spoke of his months of abstinence, how he despised and was set on beating what he called his affliction. It was heartbreaking because he was trying to deal with it alone, white-knuckling it. He had no chance. Jack London's *John Barleycorn* was a blow-by-blow history of his drinking and the failed attempts to put it behind him. He actually envisioned the program that might have helped him, but that was twenty-five years in the future he never had, dead from alcohol at forty years old.

Forty days is the time spent in Bardo, the Buddhist journey from death to rebirth. It's also the amount of days Jesus spent in the desert. That's the time your body needs to detox from whatever it is you're on, not get sober, just detox. One night at 9 p.m. I went to sleep, not the passing out I used to call sleep, real sleep, through the night, with the animals and insects and the rest of the natural life on the planet. I woke to a rooster crowing at the sun and I felt so good I thought there was something wrong with me. No need to reach in my pocket for a wake-up of drugs or a handful of aspirin, just a good feeling. I had been a Buddhist for the last eight years, but that morning was the first time I ever meditated sober. Breathing the clean air on top of that mountain, I was back to being an innocent kid riding my bike in the country, thinking about girls and football and whatever the hell else, but not about drugs or how much I'd like a drink.

I went down for breakfast and the kids saw me and they knew. They hugged and kissed me and asked for confirmation, the key word, "dormire," sleep. Some of them were still in their teens, from ghetto neighborhoods and towns like Scampia, Torre del Greco, Afragola, Forcella, Sanità. The names reek of poverty and pain, kids strung out since they were twelve, casualties of a billion-dollar drug trade, trying to make it back to themselves and a real life. For them the program is three years long, but the success rate is remarkable for those who stick it out. How long did I need, a sixty-one-year-old American filmmaker who has been using for forty-four years? Who knows, and that morning I didn't care. I was free. Free from the slavery of waiting for a dealer on some street corner, the daily grind of supporting and maintaining a habit, and the lying and cheating and thieving that goes with it. Tony made it clear to me that they would not accept Salvatore's offer to pay for my recovery. He took me in because of his responsibility to the addict, in a country that supports places like this. To the compassion of the Italian people I owe my life.

WELCOME TO NEW YORK 2

I got a message from Noémie, an angel disguised as Vincent Maraval's assistant, telling me I had to come to Paris right away. "Vincent needs you here tomorrow, please." Things don't move so fast in the south of Italy. I wasn't under lock and key, but it was a grudging ok I got from Tony to go. I am dressed in a new blue Prada suit that Dafoe hustled for me. Unlike every inconvenient airport in the world, the Napoli airport is right in the heart of the city. I guess with Vesuvius bubbling in the distance no one's sweating a plane crashing right into downtown. Francesco, once a dealer at the infamous Napoli Centrale train station, a melting pot of drug dealers from Africa to Kazakhstan, was a counselor in the program. He would drive me around for gas and cigarette money. He had never flown anywhere in his life, and today he was in charge of getting me on the plane. There was a beautiful flight attendant at the Sky priority desk. He walks right up to her and proceeds to tell her my entire life story, the people behind us screaming as they are about to miss their plane. Nobody stands in line in Napoli. There is no concept of it. People gang up on the person in control and talk and scream and jockey around, and somehow it all gets figured out. I grew up in this tradition. As a kid in the suburbs I was mortified every time I would go with my father to the grocery store or the local ice cream stand. He would just go right to the front.

I get my ticket, which Francesco holds up like we won the lottery, and we hug goodbye by the big windows overlooking the runways. That's where he stood until my plane disappeared in the sky, and that's where he was when I landed four days later. That's how people are down there. That's how I got sober.

No one was waiting at Orly. I stood at the meeting point in my blue suit, with no working phone, looking for a driver with my name on a card. I felt like an infant back out in the world. I went to rent some time on a computer and emailed Noémie who wrote back, "The driver is stuck in traffic. Just wait." None of the later films Vincent and I did together would have had a chance of getting made without Noémie. She was the smartest person in the room, so I had to believe her when she said the car was coming. Except I am one day back in the real world with no real-world skills. I felt like Gena Rowlands in Cassavetes's

Woman Under the Influence, when Peter Falk throws a party filled with family and friends to celebrate her return from a year in an insane asylum. The car came, and I made it to their office near the Pompidou in the Beaubourg.

No one in Vincent's crew seemed to notice any change in me. They were too busy with what they had going on that day. Unbeknownst to me, Vincent had spent the last year putting together a comedy with Depardieu and some other French stars. It was part three of some idiot movies based on some comic strip called *Obelix* something. I saw their posters in my peripheral vision stuck up all over town on the ride in. Now I'm right in front of the giant one hanging in the entrance to their office. Depardieu is in some ridiculous outfit with an upside-down funnel on his head, under the credit "Wild Bunch presents." Noémie and the guys explained what was going on. The first two versions made plenty at the box office, and now Vincent gambled all the company's money and god knows who else's on making the third. Vincent told me later that the profits they expected would allow us to make the films we wanted to make. You plan, God laughs, and a plan like that really cracks Him up.

By 8 p.m. of the opening night, which was to be the celebration of a whole new era for all of us, the film had tanked. It was an unqualified box office disaster. This maniac Maraval had blown 30 million dollars in less than a day.

He and I walked alone that night through Paris, toward an apartment they had set up as the distribution center for the opening, passing by his posters on every corner. I was thinking, we could have made a dozen *Welcome to New York*'s with that money. My old self would have tried to strangle him, but my recovery was in gear and I just let it go.

Upstairs the whole young team were on their computers, expecting they would be popping champagne by now instead of counting the pitiful grosses still trickling in from the provinces. Some of them, trying to make their leader feel better, said the word of mouth for the 10:30 p.m. show might save them. Yeah, sure. They all knew they would probably be driving taxis in a few days. Vincent stayed cool through all of it, you got to give him that. I asked, "You want me to stay to walk you home?" He said, "No, that's all right. We have a nine a.m. appointment at Gérard's house tomorrow. I think he found the rest of the financing for our movie." I looked at him and thought, fuck this fucking film business, fuck this "never say die" business. In this moment of absolute, utter defeat, lying across the ropes, blood flowing from everywhere, Vincent refuses the referee. He wants to fight on. He said, "Go back to the hotel and get some rest. Tomorrow we have to tell Gérard that in order to get the rest of the financing he must defer his salary." Really, so after Gérard comes up with a third of the budget, we're going to tell him he's not getting paid.

I walked back to my hotel thinking about a lot of things, but not about a drink. The obsession to use had been lifted from me, the miracle unfolding, and so I lay down in bed in the Marais and slept the sleep of a normal person.

Gérard at nine in the morning was right where I left him a year before, sitting at the big kitchen table in a room the size of a small church, this time alone. If he knew his movie had opened the previous night, he didn't mention it. Vincent wasn't there, he and his crew were off on a three-day run. The first thing Gérard said was, "What happened to you?" He was the only person to sense that something in me had changed. I told him all about the last few months, finishing with, "I can't make the film anymore. Not drinking is too important to me and I can't be around anyone who is." He answered right away. "I won't drink during the shoot."

"For five weeks straight?"

"Yes, I will do it, for you." He brought me over to a painting on the wall that his son Guillaume had done. Guy, which rhymes with key, was also an actor and a writer, and now dead, heroin playing a major role. Gérard took out more of his son's artwork and read me some of his writings. There were a lot of tears shed that morning. Why some of us make it and some of us don't is unknowable. Statistically, the chances of a long-term addict like him or me getting clean are slim to none. They call it "By the grace of God," whether you believe in Him or not. Guy was in and out of rehabs his whole life but never could get it. Gérard never gave up hope that his son would somehow make it through.

Gérard pulled $750,000 out of a guy from Azerbaijan who claimed to be a watch salesman based in Switzerland. He was a scary-looking dude, but always a gentleman. The go-between was Pascale Perez, a super-smart, super-chic woman in her late thirties. Lethal in business, she was the alpha dog of our crew. She brought the watch salesman and his 750k to Gérard. Maraval and his partner Ibrahim came off the mat with another 750k. With that, and our NYC tax credit, we were now in play, as they say in the biz.

The four months I spent in rehab without the thought of making films, or actively hustling their budgets, got me two features, *Welcome to New York* and *Pasolini.* With my self-proclaimed brilliant producing skills on ice, letting the people who actually do this for a living do their thing, these two films came to be. Panic and negativity and fear of financial insecurity were no longer my daily diet. Letting go, surrendering, is what it's called and like Kelsch says, "What is surrender but to join the winning side."

I left the rehab amidst tearful goodbyes. Tony's farewell words to me were, "If you see people you used to know, run." People, places, and things is what we call it. I was having zero to do with all three. I went to live in Paris because I never really hung out or used there. I started going daily to the English-speaking AA meetings with a whole new way of hearing what was being said. That's when Shanyn and I began drifting apart. She had waited so long for me to get straight, and now that I was, she couldn't handle me. The sex was one thing. They say your emotional development ends when you begin using and starts again when you stop, so she was basically dealing with an eighteen-year-old boy. Our life together, in a nice apartment in the Bastille, became intolerable to her. A key suggestion of the program is no big changes in the first year of sobriety. No new relationships, no breaking up of old ones, no job change, no quitting cigarettes, no crazy diets, nothing except abstinence. I was going to wait one year to leave her. She wound up leaving me two days before that. But we were finished the minute I took that last bag of dope.

We set a start date for *Welcome to New York* for the beginning of May, and with great trepidation I flew back to the city. I put a huge down payment on an overpriced apartment in Williamsburg. It was all out of my own pocket till the film account got rolling. I was not going to stay in Manhattan, way too many ghosts. Brooklyn, like Paris, was virgin territory for me. For the first time I'm living on this side of the bridge, literally under it, an all-Spanish hood that back in the day I wouldn't have been caught dead in. Now the bodegas are selling designer Italian espresso alongside the Bustelo.

We are a week away from shooting and everything is going smoothly when Jonathan, our production attorney, summons us to an emergency conference call. "No one is insuring this project with the rape scene in there." The insurance company was not too crazy about Gérard or me either, but the lawyers could get us past that. Still the bottom line, after a lot of talking, was the rape scene had to go. In this business, no insurance, no film.

I put down the phone and my mind went into overdrive. Instantly I'm in addict mode. "Fine, tell me this five days before shooting, after I just put down 25k for a deposit on an apartment in the last place on earth I want to be living." Shanyn was the only one at home, and she knew I wasn't shouting at her. I cursed out the walls, the world, and everyone in it. I wanted to trash everything around me, shit I didn't even own. I broke down in tears and then came up with the best idea I ever had in my life. "Who insures Michael Moore?"

Adam Folk, our young hotshot producer who went through the test of fire in *4:44* and came out a successful LA executive, was back for more torture as producer of *Welcome to New York.* He's a trustworthy dude, and with his Wayfarers on he's the spitting image of John Kennedy, so he's our perfect front man. He hears me out as I tell him, "I mean Michael Moore just goes and knocks on someone's door with the camera rolling, and if they don't pull a gun they keep filming. Who insures that?"

It turns out the guy who insures Michael Moore's movies works out of a storefront in Kansas City. Thirty-six hours later Adam found him and got him the script. He read it and agreed to insure it in principle. He needed one conversation before we closed the deal. Another conference call. The same LA and NYC lawyers, Maraval and Ibrahim connected in from Paris. Our insurance salesman, whose only experience in the film business was Moore's films, had that slow-talking Midwest twang, but he had done his homework. "This is one hell of a story. How do you know it's all true?" Now it's up to me to do the talking. One wrong word and four years of planning and $3 million in investments go down the fucking drain. "Court documents," I tell him. "Verified emails."

"And the wife, you think she might give us any trouble?" He got the picture. He went right to the heart of it. I told him what I had learned. "She knew everything."

"Wow," he said. "That's some broad."

We got the insurance. A few frantic days later it's day one of principal photography. We could no longer use *DSK* as the title, which would have been my choice, because I like them short and sweet. Driving across the Williamsburg Bridge heading into Manhattan as it becomes Delancey Street there is a small sign that says, "The Borough President," whatever his name was, "Welcomes You to New York." Ok, now we got the title.

It's the first time I have directed sober since I was a kid. I showed up early figuring I would ease into it. Gérard was already there. He had set up shop right in the middle of the lobby, which was the set for that day. I had made sure that he had a dressing room and a cool trailer, but he never stepped foot in either. He never left the set for five weeks. He was there early and stayed late. He fed off the process, blossomed, and through him I reconnected to the joy of filmmaking. "Engage with your people, revel in the chaos," as Dafoe likes to say. "Use all that."

Gérard was still in his underwear, eating eggs and drinking coffee and getting into it with our crew and Turid, his personal makeup woman we brought over from France. He had immediately developed a rapport with Kenny and his whole camera department. He had the prop guys working for him, writing his lines of dialogue on giant white cards. Chris Zois was right next to him doing the final rewrite. "Doctor, please, this line I cannot say." Chris would take it out or rewrite it on the spot. "Doctor, please forgive me, but this line maybe should change like this," and so it went until they filled three or four more cards. I am standing with Kelsch and we are not happy. "Where are we going to put that shit?" Our methodology was to load up two cameras, say or don't say "action," and let it rip for about twenty minutes. Do that a few times and there's the scene. We are not setting up shots, we are following actors, shooting 360 degrees. So where are these fucking cards going? When Kenny gets that skeptical look, the crew knows it's time for me to start to direct. The soundman had offered Gérard an earwig, a device you put in your ear so someone can feed you your lines, a method Brando made famous. I went back with the soundman to make a last desperate plea to Gérard. "The makeup fixes it so the camera doesn't see it and the continuity person will read you the lines. It works great."

"Ah-bel, please I cannot use this. The script person speaks, then they begin to act, and then I cannot think. It is impossible." I am there to help, not argue, so fine. Gérard didn't make 250 films for nothing. He was there early for a reason, not just to bullshit with the crew but to watch where they put the lights and where Kenny set the dollies. He knew how we planned to attack that room and he knew where those cards had to go. We never saw one during the whole shoot.

Gérard was playing the head of the International Monetary Fund but he looked more like a Hells Angel I once knew from San Jose. That Angel is dead but his spirit lives in Gérard, who also has been known to knock guys out who fucked up his Harley. The thought of putting a tie around his neck, if you could find one big enough, was a joke.

The shooting began. We scheduled the scene of the rape for day two. Day one was the orgy stuff. We had a female-heavy NYC union crew, whose rep, our boom operator, told us she would stop work if we didn't provide a bathroom on the floor we were shooting on. Union regulations. An hour later she's holding the boom to get the best sound as one of my actresses is licking the other one's pussy.

We ended late that first night with everyone feeling the vibe that something good was happening. Gérard was giving and alive and one of us. I needed to see that because I needed to know I could come back to doing my thing without the shit. Rolling with my best friends, a sixteen-year-old with his uncle's movie camera, not under the influence of anything but the love of making movies, sleeping on the set, sharing pizzas, the whole troupe in it together.

I was heading home through Tribeca up West Broadway when someone stepped out of the shadows. It was Maraval, the last person I expected, but I was happy to see him. By this point Gérard had announced that if he saw him again he was gonna knock him out. I didn't know why, and I didn't ask, but that's why Vincent didn't come to the set for his usual visit. So we talked in the dark. It was about the rape scene. He was making his final plea for me not to shoot it. It was a legal issue. "For the sake of the project, for the sake of our companies, our families, don't do it." I wasn't going to argue our wack insurance policy or my contractual final cut or anything. It was something beyond that. The right of personal expression does not cover it either. It is our DNA. You can't spend your life worshipping at the feet of Cassavetes, Fassbinder,

Godard, Billie Holiday, and Keith Richards, and be planning a film on Pasolini, and back off of this scene. The Hippocratic Oath, I can do the patient no harm. When the film is being harmed, I cannot let it happen, never, that's my oath as a director. But give Vincent credit, he flew all the way to New York to make his case. He went back to Paris the next morning. We began shooting the scene.

Susan Batson is a great acting coach and teacher. I knew her from Juliette Binoche when we all worked on *Mary*. Like Penny Allen, they are the people I go to when we are looking for actors. So when Susan told me she had the perfect girl to play Diallo, we just cast her. Maybe I saw a photograph. She was from West Africa. We met for the first time right before the take. She was already in the maid's costume. I asked if she knew what was going on and she said she did. I told her to ring the doorbell and, right from Diallo's testimony, ask, "Is anyone there?"

During final touch-ups Depardieu, who starts the scene in the shower, dropped his robe casually in front the whole crew, did a delicate pirouette on one foot, and cut a fart that shook the room. I saw the soundwoman adjust the mic level down. "Ah-bel, excuse me, but you cannot hold this in during a rape scene."

When it's time to do these scenes, Modine and Béatrice in *Blackout*, Asia and Willem in *New Rose*, or the Harvey stuff in *Bad Lieutenant*, it's always the same.

With a skeleton crew, Kenny with kneepads on to get low, the faint sound of the camera rolling the only cue for the actors. Maybe you get two takes, maybe only one, but all you need is one.

Vincent saw the film for the first time at the Wild Bunch office in Paris. It's their tradition to screen movies in a funky little room with the projection thrown up on a wall, light coming through the windows, half of them on their phones. It was a nightmare. His coterie of female executives couldn't have hated it more. I should have been there but my flight was late leaving Kennedy and by the time I got through the Parisian morning traffic they had already consolidated their notes, the one process I hate most in this business. I met up with Vincent at a cafe so I could hear his take on the feedback alone. The film was so far from everyone's expectations that there was nothing to talk about. My crying that they saw it with the wrong screen ratio or lack of proper sound rang empty even to my ears.

The elephant in the room, many different rooms but the same elephant, was final cut. I have final cut, contractually, spiritually, and with a major precedent, especially between Vincent and myself. In Europe it's a law, an actual civil, legal right that the director's work cannot be changed. It's part of the culture, a respect for art and artists, and that's the reason I live and work in Europe, but I have worked in American TV and on films without final cut, so I know what it's like to be another chump on the assembly line. *Cat Chaser,* which could have been an interesting version of a wonderful novel, ended up a travesty. A VHS copy of Tony Redman's first cut with a temp dub, found in a cardboard box somewhere, is all that remains of what could have been. After that, except for the *Body Snatchers* studio experiment, I never worked without final cut again. No matter where the financing is coming from the cut is not negotiable. In the course of a film there are millions of decisions made, and the ability to override the ones you do not think are right is what makes you the director and the film a film. It's not a free-for-all with everyone and their mother's opinion.

A contract is one thing, then there's the personal responsibility of dealing with your friend and partner, whose creative and executive team are up in arms over what they just saw. The heartache was Vincent not liking the film. We were at an impasse. I went back to NYC.

My editor Tony, as usual, is barely listening to me, never mind what anyone outside the editing room has to say. We finished the film our way and I submitted it to the Venice Film Festival. They liked it and wanted to show it in competition. It was the middle of August and we had to let them know right away if we would accept.

Vincent arrived in town with Noémie and we all had lunch at a new upscale bistro on 14th in the newly gentrified Meat Market. Our producer Adam was there, and like Noémie he was adept at keeping things moving and keeping everyone from killing each other. Zois was also there. Maraval arrived from his meeting at IFC, our American distributor, and after the pleasantries and the ordering he laid out his master plan, which had already been ok'd by them. "Do you know what pay-per-view is?"

"Yeah, it's how they put prizefights on television."

"Well we're putting together a pay-per-view deal for the whole world. IFC will do the domestic and we'll set up the international side. When the film plays at Cannes it will be broadcast simultaneously around the world." That got everyone's attention. Then he went for the kill. "It will be set up so all proceeds go through one bank account." That's the theory of the pay-per-view platform, all the proceeds from the sale of each individual view, anywhere in the world, come into the same account, ours. In my experience whenever people sit around a table and talk like this someone ends up in jail, and one of us still might.

The law of my jungle is a film gets put out there as soon as it's done. The longer you wait, the longer some tragedy can occur. Leaving a finished film on the shelf for the better part of a year, waiting for the next Cannes Film Festival, is not a good idea. This plan threw the Venice premiere three weeks away right out the window, and never mind that we hadn't even screened it for Thierry Frémaux of Cannes. But details like that meant nothing to Vincent.

Zois loved the idea. The other side of his doctor/author/screenwriter persona is a high roller, who has lived through schemes and dreams and house arrests. So he says, "What's a year? In fact Cannes is only nine months away." Adam and Noémie just listened and I for once did the same. It wasn't likc there was a vote anyway. In a small act of defiance I picked up the overpriced check, kissed everybody goodbye, and headed back to Brooklyn.

Walking down 14th Street toward the L train I am talking out loud like a madman, not giving a fuck how crazy I look. "And what are we going to do when all this theoretical money comes in to this one mythical bank account? Buy a spaceship and fly to the fucking moon?"

Back at home Shanyn was unraveling. She was still attending Buddhist teachings and had her yoga practice, but she was also deep into the shamanistic realm, masters, spells, crystals, healers, all things foreign to me. I was trying to keep it simple, practical, boots on the ground, hitting a meeting with Tony every day before going to the cutting room. Working for a living was never her thing and interacting with the world was always strictly on her terms, two traits I have been attracted to before and since. Was I enabling this behavior? After starring in *4:44*, she was basically a day player in *Welcome to New York*, and in my next movie *Pasolini* she had no role at all. I'm sure that wasn't helping, but there was more going on. I emerged from rehab the same troubled, fucked-up person. The journey to becoming a loving, caring boyfriend does not take four months or four years for that matter, that's what the one day at a time thing is about. Like Springsteen sings, it's "one step up and two steps back."

Shanyn took off in the middle of the night while I was sleeping. She spent everything she had staying alone at a suite in some five-star hotel in Williamsburg, so she didn't have the money to pay the cab that brought her to JFK. She imagined she had an appointment with Johnny Depp in London. She didn't even have a plane ticket. She contacted Dr. Zois, who was helping her during this period. He talked the driver out of calling the police and covered the cab fare with his American Express card. Thankfully Milos Forman's wife Martina, Shanyn's dear friend, sent a car to pick her up and bring her to their house in Connecticut. After a day of scaring Martina and poor Milos, Shanyn came back to our apartment in Brooklyn and stayed inside for a week staring into a crystal and running up hundreds of dollars talking to some spiritualist on a 900 number. She had dropped the Gypsy woman out of the blue about a year earlier, but she was still in need of having the future predicted for her. I have no skills when it comes to a real psychiatric situation, so when she threw a half-filled bottle of organic something from the second-floor balcony, just missing my head and shattering at my feet, it was time to call her mother. Her parents arrived that night and while her poor father and I stood outside in the hall, a shriek from *The Exorcist* came from inside, commanding her mother to leave. Shanyn needed the care of a professional and it was from the guidance and help of Dr. Zois that she was able to emerge from that darkness. He had done it before for Marla. It's his gift. Years later, when I explained to our spiritual teacher Phuntsok that the relationship with Shanyn ended just as I got sober, he said, "Well, her job was finished."

It was the first week in September and time for me to go to Rome and begin prepping *Pasolini.* The SUV to the airport was waiting in front of the new apartment I hooked up for us in Fort Greene. I got in, not realizing that my days of calling NYC home were over, and except for a few days that Christmas, I would never see Shanyn again.

PASOLINI

HARRY

CRISTINA

We first heard about Pasolini at university. I was going to Purchase, less than an hour from the city, and living in the country north of there. This was when you couldn't dial up a movie on your laptop. Information was word of mouth and mysteries were rampant. You could only see movies like Pasolini's at the Regency or the Thalia in Manhattan, or at one of the colleges with a film program. New York had plenty of them, but most were all the way the fuck up in Siberiaesque places like Binghamton or Rochester or worse. I forget which one *Accattone* was rumored to be playing at, but a bunch of us jammed in a VW Bug to go. We didn't get far. Snow was falling, and between a funky heater and bald tires we had to turn back, dejected. But Harry was not to be denied. He said, "I got to see this movie." He left with a baggie of cheap pot and a jug of even cheaper red wine stuffed in his shoulder bag. We watched through the windows as he walked into a blizzard toward the highway to hitch a ride hundreds of miles north.

I met Harry when we were teenagers. He lived nearby but went to a Catholic school, so it was the summers that I got the full dose. He had crazy long black hair and a scraggly, not-quite-there beard, and always wore cutoff jeans with combat boots, even in the winter. No one looked anything like him. He was also a chick magnet. They adored this maniac and he taught us why. He would preach the importance of buying flowers and presents, worshipping their birthdays, listening closely when they spoke.

A week later he showed up back at the house. He had made it there too late for the *Accattone* screening, but he tracked down the projectionist, asleep in his dorm room, and in exchange for the weed and the wine the guy took him back to the theater and ran the movie for him.

Harry acted out the whole film for us as we passed around joints and watched him impersonate Franco Citti and the rest of the young Roman street thugs. My passion for this person named Pier Paolo Pasolini was ignited, and when *The Decameron,* his latest film, came to 59th and Third Ave we raced down and got to see the master in action. Being Italian American is one thing, to see the real ones in their natural habitat was mind-blowing. The filmmaking loose, free-form, easy, the great Tonino Delli Colli's miraculous mix of natural light with his own instruments catapulted you to another world. How the fuck do you do this? When we realized later on it was Pasolini himself playing Giotto's pupil, that clinched it for me. Godard was my man, but now it was all things Pasolini. We devoured everything we could find about him, even met someone at film school who had assisted him for a summer who we tortured for information. Then, in 1975, he got killed. If he was a god before, he now entered another dimension of coolness. James Dean crashing his sports car, Morrison, Janis, and Hendrix all doping out was one thing, but getting run over by your own trick on some overgrown strip of beach past the Rome airport, that wins the prize.

When asked his occupation for a visa or other official documents he would just put down "Writer." Writer, director, journalist, poet, political activist, that was the message. Directing films is only a part of it, not all of it.

The research for our movie brought me in touch with his most intimate friends and family. My screenwriter Maurizio Braucci and I heard the message over and over. Pasolini was a man of compassion and commitment, full of love. On the set he treated everyone with kindness, down to the youngest assistants.

Salò, his last feature, is so far outside the box it's from another galaxy. We were at the American premiere up on 57th Street. It was a long movie so we came with wine and bread and cheese. There were fifteen people in the theater and when it ended there were eight. To this day I am still in contact with two of them because of that shared experience. We stood under the marquee and just looked at each other, no one saying a word. It was night now and it had begun to snow, but who cared, I didn't even know what city I was in.

At the time of his death Pasolini had already written his next two films, the first of which was the story of Saint Paul, using biblical language but reimagined during the Nazi occupation of Paris, and ending in a room full of Black Panthers in 1968 Detroit. Who knows what he would have done with that. His other unrealized script, PORNO-THEO-KOLOSSAL, was to star Eduardo De Filippo as one of the three wise men who followed the star to Bethlehem, a story told many times, except Pasolini imagines the conversation the wise man had with his wife before leaving.

WIFE Where you going?
KING To be at the birth of the Messiah.
WIFE What messiah, where?
KING I don't know where, that's why I'm following the star.
WIFE What star? Stay home, stop drinking.

The king's trip brings him to a Rome of the future, with '50s cars and deco clothes, a city that is entirely gay. Anyone arriving from the outside is checked out by the gay cops waiting at the train station, and if you're straight you're directed to Prati, the rich section of Rome across the river. How does the race procreate in an all-gay world? Pasolini imagines a feast day based loosely on the pagan ritual dedicated to the gods of fertility that happens to fall on Mardi Gras, nine months before Christmas. The guys put up their best men and the women theirs. It's not so much an orgy as a strategy, knock up as many chicks as possible, one at a time, as fast as possible, the women screaming "cazzo cazzo cazzo," dick dick dick, the men screaming "fica, fica," pussy pussy, drums banging and fireworks going off on each orgasm. How could you not try to put that on film?

For the first time, Pasolini narrated his script into a cassette tape recorder instead of writing it down. The tape is a treat, ninety minutes of pure story, a blueprint for the crew who would have to shoot it.

Then came the night we actually had to pull this off. The casting had come up with plenty of young Italian studs, some of whom were crew members, all assuring me they could keep it up even in a blizzard. Well it wasn't quite a blizzard that night, but it was unseasonably cold and the location we chose was outdoors, up in the hills outside Rome. Willem had made a hundred-dollar side bet with me that my actors would not be able to perform when they heard action. We brought plenty of Viagra and electric heaters that night, because you are not making a Pasolini movie filming limp dicks. The women were told to watch *Salò* and be ready for anything. The ones who were our friends didn't need to be told.

Cristina was a university student living with her mother, reading Keats and Shelley in English and Dostoevsky in Russian. They were from Moldavia, which was part of the USSR. She was born right before glasnost, and was crowned Miss Moldavia as a teenager before she left for Italy to be with her mother. She came on a blind casting and Gabriella, our casting director, hired her on the spot. She was explained the Triple X deal and told to be at the address at 6 p.m. She had second thoughts at the last minute and almost didn't show, but her Russian mother, who is as liberated and hardworking as they come, told her, "Just go, you never know who you might meet. If you don't like it, come home."

A merkin is a wig for your pussy. Being that the movie within the movie was 1975, all the girls were being fitted when I showed up, with Gabriella and our producer Costanza Coldagelli on either side of me. We needed to pick the Queen of the Feast of Fertility. I already had my gorgeous young King. It took about one second to choose Cristina. When the moment of truth came and the camera rolled, she blew us all away. There are people born for the camera and those who are the reason cameras were invented in the first place.

Everyone in the cast was game, but being up for it and knowing what a scene is really about are two different things. This night took everything I had, starting with trying to explain the subtlety that this is not an orgy but a necessity to further the race. Try getting that across in two languages. When we got to the first of hopefully many orgasms, the crowd cheering and hugging each other, the fireworks guy set them all off at once. I'm screaming, "Stop, we got a bunch more to go," in straight Bronxese. Too late. I kept the screaming going all night, at the actors, the crew, the drummers, the gods, until the sun came up. What we got, we got. Thankfully it was the last day of the shooting week.

In Italy goodbye is not a casual act. Everyone was bonding and double kissing and Cristina, out of makeup, hair pulled back and dressed in jeans, was back to her university student persona. I was thinking, "You cannot just let that woman leave." A director cannot be coming on to the people he's working with, that's an absolute no. After the film is over and everyone returns to their civilian life, maybe, but during, no. She came up to me to thank me and say goodbye. I thanked her the same as every one of the other actors that morning, except with her I wrote my number on a piece of paper and said, “Call me if you want.” She said, “When?” It was a Saturday morning so I said, “Sunday.”

“When?”

“Three p.m.” It was Palm Sunday, that I remember. At two minutes past three the phone rang. Four months later she was pregnant with Anna and we were both overjoyed.

WELCOME TO NEW YORK 3

ANNA

I don't like guns to begin with. Now I find myself in an empty apartment with Dr. Zois and the guy who was introduced to us as our chauffeur stretched out in a chair by the door, the handle of his piece sticking out over his belt. I am thinking what kind of chauffeur wears jeans and a leather jacket and speaks in a Russian accent.

All the principals were to meet at Depardieu's house the day before for a big summit. I flew in from Rome, Zois had come from New York, and our producers from Geneva. Vincent wasn't part of the party because Gérard was still claiming he would kill him on sight. We stood there ringing his buzzer forever but no Gérard. It was the first time I'd seen our Azerbaijani financier pissed off, but not the last. We gave up and walked to Depardieu's restaurant across the street. The maître d', who I'd gotten to know, took me aside. "Your friend has been in a bad way the last few weeks." Pascale got off her phone and announced that we would all meet tomorrow at eleven at her office instead. Gérard will be there.

The next day the "chauffeur" picked up Zois and me and took us to a very expensive part of Paris I didn't even know existed, up on a hill overlooking the Champs-Élysées. We were ushered into a townhouse with a couple of big rooms, a kitchen with nothing in it, no furniture anywhere, just a long table with enough chairs for the people coming. A badly designed set for a mob hit.

It was three months earlier that I got an email from Thierry Frémaux telling me if we wanted the film in competition we would need to make certain cuts. Strange that Frémaux, head of the Cannes Film Festival, a world-class cineaste, defender of auteur cinema, would even write a letter like this. But the fact that his bullet points were identical to Maraval's made it clear who was behind it. I love Thierry, but that didn't stop me from writing back and telling him to go fuck himself.

Gérard, Pascale, and the Azerbaijani arrived at the apartment together and we sat down. Gérard was shit-faced, I mean fucked up, on a multi-day run, but he pulled it together enough to ask me to figure out a way to make everyone happy and get the film in competition. I told him it wasn't happening. He took Zois out on the balcony, took off a serious watch from his wrist, and offered it to him to get me to start thinking straight. Pascale dialed her phone, spoke in French, then told me Maraval was on his way over. I told her it would take him an hour to get here from his office in this traffic, but five minutes later Vincent walked in as if he'd been waiting in a closet downstairs. He got right down to business. He looked at the Azerbaijani, pointed at me, and said in English, "This man just cost you two million dollars." Even the chauffeur looked over at that one. Thanks Vincent. I am basically negotiable until I feel I am getting mauled. I was not changing the film.

With the competition section not happening, Maraval tried and failed to get the film into the Quinzaine section or even as a special screening. The selection committee didn't want to hear it. The French reaction to this film was not good at all. *Pasolini* was the same deal in reverse. The Italians had a problem with a film about one of their own but liked the film about the French guy. The French, who financed and appreciated *Pasolini*, were not cool with *Welcome to New York.* It has something to do with an American invading their cultural turf.

It was now the first weekend at Cannes and Vincent defied his buddies and chose the sacred first Friday night to open the film outside the festival at a local theater, all five screens, on some side street far from the Palais. They were all packed that night, it was the ticket to have, and the lesson learned was if you got the goods you don't need acceptance from a selection committee. The movie is the accreditation.

Maraval's dream of streaming the world ended up being only in France, but it was Orange, a major communications company that did it. Vincent, always searching for the ultimate event, followed up the screenings with a wild press conference on the beach and an absurd party where the guests got bathrobes, handcuffs, and prophylactics with their hand stamps. I went home early. The next morning Anne Sinclair said publicly that she puked all over her iPad while watching the film, and Orange, Wild Bunch, and I were hit with a defamation of character lawsuit from Strauss-Kahn for an astonishing amount of money.

My advice to any of you considering adopting children is go for it, it's a beautiful thing. From the moment Endira and Lucy arrived I have loved them beyond the beyond. Now I was having a child with Cristina. Seeing Anna for the first time on the sonogram of her mother's stomach sent me to the moon. Then Cristina and her birth counselor announced to me that the baby was to be born at home. What do you mean we need to buy a wading pool, and what do you mean the medical doctors will get in the way of a natural birth? There was no talking Cristina out of it. "Women have been doing it for 100,000 years without doctors and hospitals." Their concession to me was a backup hospital in case of a real emergency. Not the perfectly fine hospital a block from my house, but one on the ass end of Rome, a city famous for traffic jams, millions of tiny one-manned cars and double-decker tourist buses on roads built for chariots. Imagining the neighborhoods we had to go through to get there, I had a clear vision of sitting in the rain in bumper-to-bumper traffic, Cristina about to give birth in the back seat with her Zen homeopathic nurse. And that's exactly what happened on a rainy March 15, when the nurse finally decided we'd be better off in the hospital, the both of them screaming at the young taxi driver as we sat in total Vatican gridlock, the taxi driver screaming back, "Why didn't you call an ambulance?" Yeah, why didn't we? They told me all I needed to do that day was to stay calm. So I stayed calm. We got there just in time and Cristina had a natural childbirth. The look on her mother's face, when she arrived that night by bus from her job caring for handicapped adults, was priceless. So was the feeling in my heart.

I was living in peace in Rome with Cris and Anna when I was informed by courier that I was wanted in court in Paris to answer the defamation charges brought by Strauss-Kahn. My attorney Filomena was skeptical about me going, but ignoring shit was a tactic from my previous life. I am no longer into things hanging over my head.

DSK and Anne Sinclair were no fools. They and their formidable legal team were after Orange for big money, and me and Maraval and his partner Ibrahim were along for the ride. On a beautiful spring day in Paris I met my French lawyer, a long-haired motorcycle-jacketed dude who pulled up for lunch on his Harley. He assured me this was only going to be a formality. But when I asked him if I should wear a tie, he thought about it and then said yes. Not a good sign, although I had instinctively bought one at the airport. After lunch I got on the back of his bike and we drove to Notre-Dame. We walked up a long metal staircase attached to the side of the cathedral and into its awesome hallways. My lawyer tied up his hair and, in a reverse-Superman move, took off his leather jacket and untucked a black legal robe from his jeans, because in France the lawyers wear robes as well as the judges.

He pushed open a side door and now I am no longer in history but in a modern police precinct filled with the sort of cops you don't see on the Paris streets, young, hard-looking, determined, equipped with color-coordinated bulletproof vests and state-of-the-art SIG Sauers. The perps, every color but white, were in cuffs, also with their lawyers. Zero English being spoken. I was taken to a room and told to sit and wait for the judge. The judge? I looked at my lawyer, who maintained a confident, no problem attitude. I asked him if Vincent had been here. He said no, only Ibrahim, poor Ibrahim, the business side of the operation, low-key and quiet, always sweet, now another Arab in the system thanks to us.

The judge arrived and sat across from me at a simple desk. She was around forty and stunning, in a black robe, and spoke only a bit of English. She began by asking if I was Abel Ferrara, AKA Jimmy Laine. AKA anything sounds ominous. Now I was getting scared. Jimmy Laine is the alias I used back when I was acting in *Driller Killer* and *9 Lives,* the last time we were making movies that might get you thrown in jail. She began talking to my lawyer in French and suddenly he didn't look so confident. I couldn't help myself, so I asked, "Am I walking out of here today?"

"Oh yes, of course, Monsieur Ferrara," the judge answered. A stenographer arrived and sat to my left, a twenty-something-year-old sweetie dressed French working woman style, high heels and a black dress. Then, for my sole benefit, a translator was brought in, a feisty little American in her seventies with a heavy Chicago accent. She sat close to me, speaking in my ear as the judge read the charges in French. "They have no problem with the movie, only with one scene, at the 30-minute, 19-second mark. The maid says, 'Is anyone here?'" I knew what was coming. She continued, "He comes out of the shower naked. At the 30-minute, 44-second mark he takes the maid by the back of the neck." The judge was keeping it even-tempered. I looked over at the stenographer, who was typing while staring straight at me. The translator was putting enough drama into it that it seemed twice as sordid as what we actually shot. By the time they got to the cum shot I knew we were fucked. This was no mere formality. The translator broke the silence, saying unprompted and to no one in particular, "Sounds like some movie."

Here's a few million dollars' worth of legal advice, direct from Strauss-Kahn's high-priced American lawyer Ben Brafman. When you get caught by the cops, keep your mouth shut. I got that for free starting at three years old. "Nobody ever got in trouble keeping their fucking mouth shut." Diallo wasn't in trouble, she was the victim. She was telling her story and that's what our movie is about, her story, because no one else was telling theirs.

Welcome to New York eventually came out in the States with the edit that put in doubt Diallo's testimony, so the poor woman was betrayed again, by both IFC and Wild Bunch and the women executives who worked there, like the women in the DA's office whose recommendation was to drop the case. So if the most dangerous thing to a woman is a man, the second most dangerous thing is another woman.

IFC's deal with the cable company demanded an R-rated American release. This is a practice our editor Tony perfected back in the PG, R, NC-17 days. We even did a television version of *Bad Lieutenant.* This time I passed on it, which shows that just because you're sober doesn't mean you make the right choices. Was I hearing the ghost of Peckinpah when they offered him the opportunity to fix the butcher job that was done to *Major Dundee*, and he said, "You fucked it up, now you live with it." After Sam died someone knowledgeable did the world the favor of putting it back together right, and the great Heston performance, rivaling the one he gave Welles in *Touch of Evil*, another initially butchered film, was preserved.

The real version of *Welcome to New York* is playing out there somewhere. We have the pristine DCP and some DVDs scavenged from the editing room. It's been shown at the Museum of Modern Art, even the Louvre. Depardieu in the meantime is facing rape charges of his own, maybe sitting in the same hearing room I was in, in front of the same judge.

MIAMI VICE

TAMMY

It was 1985 when I had an affair with Tammy, a student who had just graduated from South Carolina University, a cheerleader and the star of her school plays. I met her while I was directing *Miami Vice*, one of the perks not in the fine print of the contract. She was sweet and smart and my date for the evening to the big wrap party that ended the first year of shooting, celebrating *Vice*'s takeover of the world. We were together in my hotel suite getting ready to go. I had laid a blanket out on the floor of the living room with a pillow on it because the intimacy of the bedroom scared me. I was thinking maybe I wouldn't, but in the middle of the hugging and kissing she asked, "Why are you afraid to fuck me?"

The Miami to New York flight is the best, just long enough to have a few drinks and relax. I was reading an article about a Viet vet's love affair with a Vietnamese girl on a brief R&R fling. He returned to the jungle, and after his thirteen months was up he stayed to look for her. She was gone. He went back to his hometown, lost his will to live, and, in the perfect ending for the *New Yorker* editors, wrote a note professing his love for the woman before blowing his brains out.

I had been married for three years. Nancy and I made the decision to adopt because of our inability to conceive a child together, and were waiting for Endira to arrive. Tammy was the first girl I cheated with since I began this chapter of my life, but that door opens only one way, and there's no coming back out.

I was looking down over Manhattan on the descent because you seldom land from the west. It was the Emerald City for real, sun setting, buildings gleaming, World Trade Center still towering over downtown. Sitting in the front of that plane I began to cry uncontrollably, for that dead soldier, his lover, the family I was hoping for.

People always said I was psychic, and I believed that until the code of causes and conditions was unlocked to me. Nothing is preordained. My thoughts, actions, and words determined what was to come, and you live with the consequences. But the energy, the life force you come into the world with, can be flipped from the bad back to the good, refocused and nurtured. Lama Yeshe's teaching, "The clouds are not an element of the sky." Or the Native American parable, "We all have two wolves inside of us, the evil one and the good one. Which one survives? The one you feed."

MOVIES

They say the eyes are the window to the soul and on a big screen they are the size of a two-story building. It's an easy walk in, and if there is something inside, you leave the theater feeling you know the actors better than your loved ones. There is also the black, that space between the frames. Hold up a piece of 35mm film, if you can find one, and you'll see a band of black separating each image. The film goes through the projector one frame at a time. If you stand beside it you can hear it clacking. That's the film starting and stopping 24 times a second, which your eye and mind perceive as one constant motion. But you're experiencing the black too, 1/60th of a second per frame. So in a two-hour movie the audience is sitting in the dark for more than ten minutes. Is it in those ten minutes of communal unconscious darkness that the experiences people talk about getting from *Treasure of the Sierra Madre* or *Psycho* take place? You are not getting that digitally and you may never get it again, unless shooting in negative and 35mm projection makes a big comeback.

Someone came up to Kelsch and me before the premiere of a new movie of ours and said *Driller Killer* was one of his favorite films. He told us that as a twelve-year-old boy he went to the video store and rented a bunch of G-rated movies, sticking the X-rated *Driller Killer* in the middle to get past the cashier. He went home, waited for his mother to fall asleep, then snuck downstairs to lie on the floor a foot from the TV and watch it with the sound barely on. He was still talking about it twenty-five years later. He introduced us to his wife and they went in to see the new movie. I said to Kenny, "There's no way he's topping that experience tonight."

Give them what they want, simple. But I still don't know what I want, and I don't go to a theater or a museum or a concert for what I want, I go to be blown away by what you got. No audience was expecting *2001*, or *Satyricon*, or the Stones' *Rock and Roll Circus*, or the clip of Sonny Boy Williamson singing "Nine Below Zero." That's when you get your money's worth. Giving them, whoever they are, what they want is really giving them what they have seen, because something already done can be quantified and budgeted and planned. When I got to Hollywood in the late '70s all the hip movie vets told me the accountants were taking over the business, meaning it was the end of the age of *Easy Rider* and *Midnight Cowboy* and *Fat City* and many other freewheeling winners.

The upside of today's technology for the filmmaker is complete access to the means of production and distribution, which we never had. You own an iPhone and you have a film studio in your hands. Add the internet and you have your own worldwide distribution system. That freedom is my optimism because storytelling is not going anywhere. I like to read, especially on a plane, but when I stand in the back of the cabin and see everyone who's not sleeping locked into something on the screen in front of them I know I'm in the right business.

From the beginning of man someone has been telling the tale or drawing it on a cave wall. The events that don't become stories are lost. Some of us are killing the animal, some of us are building the fire, some preparing and cooking it. And afterward some of us stand up and tell the story, scratching pictures into stone to confirm it, as proof we exist. Proof we care about sharing what we learned with another human being.

THANKS

Elisabetta Sgarbi is a very cool Italian book publisher and film director. She dresses like it's downtown Manhattan 1977 because that's her favorite year. One day she called Bruno Della Ragione, a lawyer of mine. Bruno was once Fellini's lawyer, and was adept at navigating big players through big deals in both cinema and politics. If you want to do business in Italy, both parties have to agree on one lawyer. I had to forget my American hang-up about "conflict of interest," here it's "no conflict, no interest." Filomena is a protégée of his and my day-to-day attorney, because Bruno is now beyond the petty details of legal work. Elisabetta was the Italian publisher for both Tarantino's and Oliver Stone's books, and that day she was meeting Oliver in a hotel on the Via Veneto. We met before in one of the hotel's big beautiful bars and she came right out and asked. "Would you be interested in writing a book about your life?" My usual response would have been, "How much do I get for it?" but I had promised Filomena I would leave that all up to her. I said I was already thinking about writing one.

Thinking about writing a book and having to face a blank page with hundreds to follow are two different things. I had recently written the scripts to *Tommaso* and *Zeros and Ones* alone, but both were about thirty pages long and took a year to do. At that rate I would be writing this book for the next ten years. But I took the advance and started.

Thankfully there are some good books on writing by some of my favorite authors, Gibson, T. C. Boyle, Chuck Palahniuk, and Stephen King, never mind Elmore Leonard's "10 Rules of Writing" and Hemingway's thoughts on writing culled from his books and letters. Then there's Mailer's *The Spooky Art.* Plenty of knowledge in all of them, starting with King's directive. You want to learn to write? Read. Well that I have been doing since childhood. My mother read a bit. Her favorite was Pearl S. Buck's *The Good Earth.* My father kept it to the *Daily News* and the *New York Post.* He didn't have time to be reading novels. If I have to choose between seeing a movie and reading a book there's no question I'll take the book. More bang for your buck.

The deadlines came and went but I kept working at it and after a couple of years I got to a first draft. Causes and conditions? Fate or miracles? Soon after I got an email from Sean Manning at Simon & Schuster saying that he had been in the audience in Brooklyn ten years ago when Tony Redman and I were doing a joking introduction to *Welcome to New York.* He asked if I had ever considered writing a book. Considered it? I sent him the pages and waited for a response. My composer Joe Delia and my producers Diana Phillips and Mary Kane had been reading it all along and were very encouraging. So were some of the writers I knew. But this was the publishing house of F. Scott Fitzgerald and Hemingway. Sean was the editor of Dylan's latest book *The Philosophy of Modern Song.* Three weeks went by with no reply. In my program it's called restraint of pen and tongue, which means don't go firing off emails telling people to go fuck themselves, which I still have a penchant for. I was about to write, "Yo scumbag, don't go rattling my cage and then not get back to me," when his email arrived. It was positive, thought out, and more importantly he offered me a deal.

I was intent on doing this alone, but after two years and 300 pages of shit thrown against the wall I turned to Timothy Ferris, a real writer and a dear friend who taught at Berkeley and edited for *Rolling Stone* back in the day. His son Patrick, who I've known since he was born, is a musician on the West Coast who even jams with my band when we're in town. His contribution is priceless. He would never claim to be a cowriter but I don't know another word for it. Editor maybe. Like being in the cutting room with the dailies, we took what we had and disciplined it down to get this. Sean generously gave his time to the countless rereads.

I want to thank them, and every loving soul along the way who believed in our cinema enough to offer an empty couch, gas money, a pot of coffee, a ride from here to there, a free lunch, or any of the million other things that go into making movies. Mentioned in this book or not, my crew and I are grateful to you all.

Abel Ferrara
Rome